950.4   De Lee, Nigel.
DEL
        Rise of the Asian
        superpowers from
        1945

$12.90

Editor: Catherine Bradley
Designer: Charles Matheson
Researcher: Cecilia Weston-Baker

Illustrated by Stefan Chabluk, Paul
Cooper and Rob Shone

© Aladdin Books Ltd 1987

Designed and produced by
Aladdin Books Ltd
70 Old Compton Street
London W1V 5PA

*First published in the
United States in 1987 by*
Franklin Watts
387 Park Avenue South
New York, NY 10016

ISBN 0-531-10407-9

Library of Congress Catalog
Card Number: 87-80229

Printed in Belgium

Front cover: Chinese observers at a nuclear test explosion.

CONFLICT IN THE 20th CENTURY

RISE OF THE ASIAN SUPERPOWERS

FROM 1945

NIGEL De LEE

Edited by Dr John Pimlott

FRANKLIN WATTS

New York · London · Toronto · Sydney

INTRODUCTION

EDITORIAL PANEL

Series Editor:
Dr John Pimlott, Senior Lecturer in the Department of War Studies and International Affairs, RMA Sandhurst, U.K.

Editorial Advisory Panel:
Brigadier General James L Collins Jr, US Army Chief of Military History 1970–82

General Sir John Hackett, former Commander-in-Chief of the British Army of the Rhine and Principal of King's College, London, U.K.

Ian Hogg, retired Master Gunner of the Artillery, British Army, and editor of *Jane's Infantry Weapons*

John Keegan, former Senior Lecturer in the Department of War Studies and International Affairs, RMA Sandhurst, now Defense Correspondent, *Daily Telegraph*

Professor Laurence Martin, Vice-Chancellor of the University of Newcastle-upon-Tyne, U.K.

The Author:
Nigel de Lee is Senior Lecturer in the Department of War Studies and International Affairs, RMA Sandhurst, U.K.

Asia, comprising the present-day countries of India, Pakistan, Bangladesh, Sri Lanka, China, Taiwan, North and South Korea and Japan, has been a center of conflict throughout the 20th century. The causes have been varied. In China the spread of communism was opposed, leading to a long period of civil war which the communists, following Mao Tse-tung's ideas of revolutionary struggle, eventually won. In Korea there was a major conflict between the forces of North and South, also part of the fight between communists and non-communists. Elsewhere splits between Muslim and Hindu (in India/Pakistan) and Buddhist and Hindu (in Sri Lanka) led to friction because of deep differences of religious belief. Territorial clashes, particularly on the borders of China and of India, have produced periodic wars, characterized by very brief campaigns. When it is added that certain countries, notably India, Pakistan and Bangladesh, also suffer the problems of rapid population growth and poverty, the reasons for conflict are easier to understand.

Yet the region does contain its success stories. Since 1945, Japan has followed a deliberate policy of non-violence, preferring to gain power and influence through economic rather than military means. India, despite internal problems, has maintained its position as the "largest democracy in the world." China, having survived civil and border wars, is beginning to emerge as a modern, industrialized country, enjoying the prestige its size and population demand.

Problems remain – tension between North and South Korea constantly threatens to break into war. India, Sri Lanka and, to a lesser extent, Pakistan and Bangladesh, continue to suffer internal friction, leading to violence and even civil war. The superpowers (the United States and the Soviet Union) wait in the wings, ready to intervene if necessary. But signs may be found to suggest that the era of conflict is passing. If that should happen, Asia has the potential to acquire a strength and prestige which until now was confined to the power blocs of East and West.

DR JOHN PIMLOTT *Series Editor*

During the upheavals of the Cultural Revolution in China, banners exhorting the people to "Strive for an even bigger victory" were put up in Peking in 1971. Slogans and official pronouncements were displayed to promote enthusiasm for Mao Tse-tung's ideas and encourage a desire for change.

CONTENTS

DISCARD

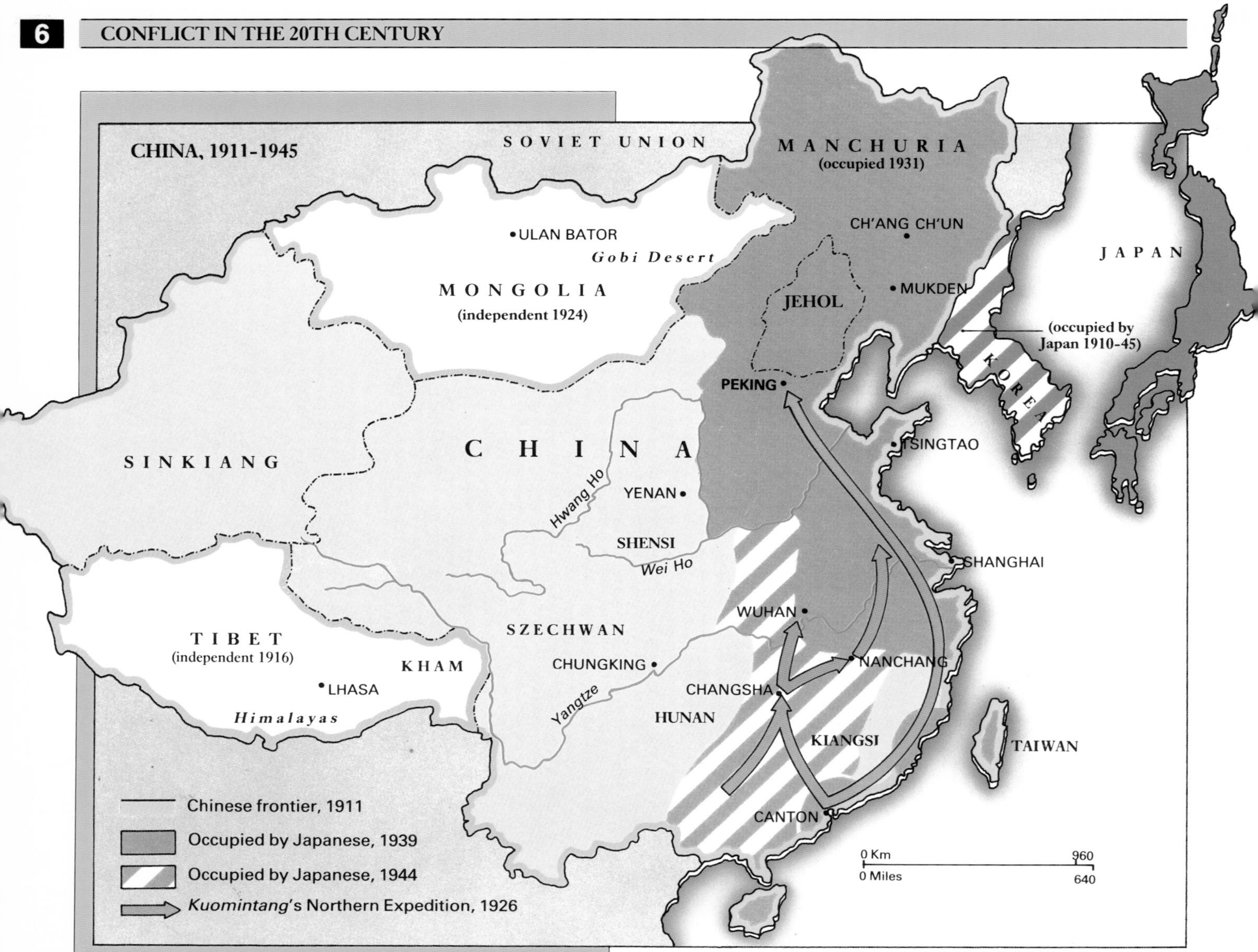

CHINA, 1911-1945

SOVIET UNION

MANCHURIA
(occupied 1931)

CH'ANG CH'UN

JAPAN

•ULAN BATOR
Gobi Desert

MONGOLIA
(independent 1924)

JEHOL

• MUKDEN

(occupied by
Japan 1910-45)

PEKING •

SINKIANG

C H I N A

•TSINGTAO

Hwang Ho

YENAN •

SHENSI
Wei Ho

SHANGHAI

TIBET
(independent 1916)

WUHAN •

KHAM

SZECHWAN

•LHASA

CHUNGKING •

Himalayas

Yangtze

CHANGSHA •

• NANCHANG

HUNAN

KIANGSI

TAIWAN

CANTON •

	Chinese frontier, 1911
	Occupied by Japanese, 1939
	Occupied by Japanese, 1944
→	*Kuomintang*'s Northern Expedition, 1926

0 Km   960
0 Miles   640

CHAPTER 1
THE MAOIST REVOLUTION

Between 1911 and 1949 China was torn apart by the effects of revolution and war. The overthrow of the last of the Emperors in 1911 led to the emergence of warlords who defied the central government, while outside powers, chiefly from Europe, controlled the major ports. New political parties were formed, notably the Nationalists and the communists. Japan took advantage of the situation to invade Manchuria in 1931, pushing deep into China itself six years later, and a full-scale war ensued. By the time of Japan's defeat in 1945, the Nationalists were weak, opening the way to a series of communist offensives which succeeded four years later.

China is an enormous country, covering an area of nearly 10 million square km (4 million square miles) and has almost unlimited economic and human potential. Situated to the southeast of Russia and the north of the India-South Asia landmass, it has traditionally acted as a source of great trading wealth, drawn from territories of tremendous diversity.

The country contains just about every type of terrain, from the awesome mountains of the Himalayas in the south to the vast Gobi Desert in the north. The population – currently put at over one billion – is drawn from a wide variety of races and peoples. However, China has a long history of civilization, with evidence of sophisticated forms of social organization and culture dating back many thousands of years.

Confucianism

In the past, China was drawn together as a nation by the evolution of unique religious and secular beliefs, most notably Buddhism and Confucianism. The latter, based on the philosophy of the ancient Chinese scholar Confucius, helped to produce a sense of resignation and deep conservatism which allowed the development of strong government. Chinese peasants traditionally accepted their place in an elaborate hierarchy of power which culminated in the divine person of the Emperor. Although opposition could (and often did) arise, the form of government survived. Such a continuity of rule, dating back to about 2200 BC, led many Chinese to regard themselves as far superior to surrounding ethnic groups. This, in turn, was often translated into policies of territorial expansion or political influence.

But the Confucian model of civilization found it difficult to adapt to new economic and political conditions. By the middle of the 19th century the old order was brutally disrupted by a series of huge rebellions which left large areas of the country in ruins. As the Chinese economy was based on agriculture, this was a mortal blow to the economic life of the country and to the finances of the central government. The Manchu emperors began to lose control.

The end of the Chinese emperors

The weakness of the country was ruthlessly exploited by foreign powers greedy for trade. Along the coast, the British, French and Americans demanded an end to the Manchu policy of isolation and the introduction of a policy of free entry for manufactured goods, merchants and missionaries. At the same time, along the frontier in the north, the Russians extended their influence by means of diplomacy, bribery and intimidation.

Each concession was another blow to the prestige of the Emperor, gradually weakening his control of the central authority and adding to a store of popular discontent. By the end of the 19th century, the central government no longer controlled many of the remote provinces, allowing local governors and senior military officers to assume greater independence. They emerged as local rulers in their own right; known as warlords, they often imposed their authority in provincial areas by means of force, raising their own armies, imposing their own taxes and ignoring the central government. By 1911, when the last Emperor – an infant aged two – was finally deposed, China had no effective government at all. Some areas of the country were controlled by foreign powers and others by cliques of warlords.

Chinese troops fighting Anglo-French forces in 1900 during a Chinese uprising against foreign powers.

The Nationalists

Meanwhile, the failure of the Emperor's rule had led to great turmoil and misery among the masses. It also inspired Chinese intellectuals to think in terms of new political ideas. These factors led to the birth of modern political movements. The first of these was the *Kuomintang* (Nationalists) led by Dr Sun Yat-sen. He believed that Chinese politics had to be based on three principles: nationalism (by which he meant an end to European exploitation and the unification of the Chinese people), democracy (based on the gradual evolution, under the *Kuomintang*, of government elected by the people) and what he called "livelihood" (the welfare of the ordinary people).

By 1911, the Nationalists were strong in the south of the country – five years later, Dr Sun was to become president of a new republic in that part of China – but in the north, the warlords were still in control. Faced with such opposition, Dr Sun decided to use the ordinary people to spread his ideas, creating a mass movement which, when armed, would be able to unite China by force.

He was also much impressed by the success of the 1917 Bolshevik revolution in Russia, particularly the organization of "cells" within the discontented urban masses, and this structure became a central feature of the new *Kuomintang* movement. Although Dr Sun's ideas were radical, he never accepted communism – the ideal of a classless society based on the common ownership of industry and property. He regarded it as entirely unsuited to the needs of China, which was a mainly agricultural country.

The communists

Not everyone agreed, for in 1921 the Chinese Communist Party was formed as a direct copy of that which had enjoyed success in Russia. Under the guidance of Michael Borodin, sent to Peking by the Bolshevik government of Russia, Chinese intellectuals were persuaded to form their own Communist Party, which would use any discontent among rootless and exploited workers to bring about a revolution.

Unlike the *Kuomintang*, the communists distrusted the ordinary peasants from the countryside, viewing their traditions of Confucianism as a dangerously conservative influence, but this did not prevent them from supporting Dr Sun in the early days. For his part, Dr Sun accepted communists into his movement, for he believed that communist ideas would be unacceptable to the Chinese peasantry.

Chiang Kai-shek and the Communist Party

Dr Sun died in 1925, to be succeeded by the Commander of the *Kuomintang* armies, Chiang Kai-shek. Chiang placed greater emphasis on military action than politics, and was less tolerant of the communists. In 1926 a period of civil and external war began; China was to be a theater of extensive military operations from then until 1949. The parties involved in this war were the warlords, the *Kuomintang*, the communists and the Japanese, with the Soviet Union and the United States as marginal participants. In 1926 the *Kuomintang* armies advanced north against the forces of the warlords, winning victory after victory.

By 1928 the warlords had been destroyed or forced to join the *Kuomintang*, and Chiang was installed in Peking as President of the Chinese Republic. To complete his work he had two major tasks: to drive the Japanese out of China and to eliminate the communists. However, he was unable to unite his own movement in support of this belief, and thus he was not able to accomplish either task.

Chiang had purged the communists from the *Kuomintang* in 1926, during the Northern Expedition. The communist leaders, following Russian advice, led a series of uprisings in the main cities, all of which failed. These failures provided scope for the development of a new theory of communist revolution based on the rural masses.

A warlord supporter is held by Kuomintang *troops, 1926.*

Mao Tse-tung (on horseback) leads his supporters during fighting in their base area of Shensi, 1947.

Mao Tse-tung's ideas

The chief author of these radical ideas was Mao Tse-tung, an educated activist from Hunan province. Although an early member of the Chinese Communist Party, he was convinced that revolution based upon the urban workers was doomed to failure (chiefly because China contained too few industrialized cities). He thought that the only hope for success lay in the peasants of the countryside. If their discontent, resulting from their pitiless exploitation by the warlords and representatives of a failing central government, could be tapped, they would represent an unstoppable mass force for change.

Once the urban risings of the 1920s had failed and the pro-Russian leadership of the Communist Party had been killed or forced into exile by Chiang Kai-shek, Mao was one of the few active revolutionaries left, and this allowed his ideas to flourish. While the *Kuomintang* armies were busy in the north, he began to set up revolutionary base areas – converting the peasants to his ideas – in remote areas in the south.

As soon as he created such bases, the local people were organized into armed groups to protect their new-found ideas. Since they lacked weapons or training, they adopted the techniques of guerrilla warfare, ambushing their opponents and gradually wearing down their resolve to destroy the base areas.

It was to take time for these ideas to evolve, but their appeal was strong. By 1930, a number of communist base areas had been established, particularly in the remote area of south Kiangsi province, and Chiang was sufficiently alarmed to mount a series of so-called Extermination Campaigns against them.

The Long March

Unfortunately, in 1934, Mao's leadership was undermined by more traditional communist activists, many of whom returned from exile when they heard of Mao's success. They watched helpless as the guerrillas had to stand and fight, pinned down by Chiang's advantages of firepower and improved tactics. In October 1934, Mao led the bulk of his followers in a desperate breakout from encirclement by the *Kuomintang*. This became known as the Long March, and lasted until October 1935, ending in the remote mountains of Shensi province in the northwest of China.

Over 100,000 communists marched nearly 9,000 km (5,500 miles) over extremely rough terrain, fighting endless battles against *Kuomintang* units for more than a year. At the end of that time, with Mao far away from the main population areas, the communist menace seemed to have been checked; in reality, it was just the beginning of a new revolutionary force, developed and strengthened by Mao in the remote safe base of Shensi.

Fighting the Japanese

Chiang was certainly in favor of continuing the pursuit of the communists, but there was another, more immediate menace. The Japanese, surprised and alarmed at the success of the *Kuomintang* and wary of the prospect of a united China, had invaded Manchuria in 1931, seizing the main industrialized area of China. Because of this, Chiang could not concentrate on defeating the communists, even during the campaign of 1934-35. Indeed, by that time, he was facing a war on two fronts, for in 1933 the Japanese invaded the province of Jehol, probing south and forward as far as the outskirts of Peking.

In such circumstances, the communist threat seemed the lesser of the two evils and in 1936 Chiang was forced by his senior military commanders to accept a "united front" with Mao's forces against the invading Japanese. Even so, the combination of *Kuomintang* and communist units was too weak to hold the Japanese when they mounted their main attack in 1937. The best of the *Kuomintang* forces were destroyed in hard fighting and the remnants retreated to the southwest, unable to take action in the war.

The Japanese went on to conquer the whole of the coastal plain and to dominate the great river valleys. The communists organized guerrilla attacks, but Mao used the opportunity to consolidate his political support among the peasants in areas under his control. His few large-scale encounters with the Japanese were generally unsuccessful and were punished by vicious reprisals. After 1941 the communists conserved their strength and prepared for the renewal of fighting against the *Kuomintang* once the Japanese had gone.

The attitudes of the superpowers

Both the United States and Soviet Union were interested in the future of China, but neither was able to devote major resources to Chinese affairs. The Soviets gave some help to the Chinese Communist Party, but were suspicious of Mao because his ideology differed so fundamentally from that of the Soviet model. The Soviet leader, Josef Stalin, did not believe that peasants could be good communists.

In 1945 the United States tried to promote a compromise between the *Kuomintang* and the communists to create a joint government to reconstruct the shattered Chinese economy. But American observers were disturbed by the *Kuomintang* intolerance of political opponents. Therefore, the United States would not give Chiang full support early in the Civil War.

Chinese peasants look on passively as Japanese troops march by, November 1938.

After the atomic bombing of Hiroshima in August 1945, the Soviets attacked and overran the Japanese army in Manchuria. They then assisted the communists in a plan to seize control of this area, and to take the military equipment of the defeated Japanese. Stalin was not in favor of Mao's plan for a final armed struggle to destroy the *Kuomintang*; he proposed that China be temporarily divided, with the *Kuomintang* ruling the south, and a communist People's Republic in the north.

But in 1945 neither Chiang nor Mao was in a mood to compromise or cooperate. Both were determined to settle the question of who should rule China, and their powerful friends could not restrain them. Chiang hoped that by strong and successful military action he could attract American support and finally wipe out the communists. Mao was determined to fight to the finish with or without Soviet help, and was confident that over the years his followers would grow stronger while the *Kuomintang* became weaker.

The state of the *Kuomintang*

In contrast, the *Kuomintang* was unprepared and unfit for civil war. Chiang was confident of his ability to unite China by force, believing that the United States would support him. But the years of defeat and inactivity had made the *Kuomintang* corrupt and inefficient.

The *Kuomintang* Army was of mixed quality. There were some 39 Central divisions of committed Nationalists, which were reliable and well supplied with American equipment. The rest, however, were unreliable formations starved of equipment. Compared to the communist troops, *Kuomintang* soldiers were badly disciplined, poorly led and demoralized. They were susceptible to communist influence, and large numbers deserted or defected to join the communists during the Civil War.

The *Kuomintang* command structure was both over-centralized and too complicated. It was designed to concentrate power in the hands of Chiang and his loyal friends in the so-called Whampoa Clique (made up of officers trained at the Whampoa military academy), and was unable to control operations efficiently.

Unlike the communists, the *Kuomintang* had no plan to put into effect once the Japanese surrendered. However, like Mao, Chiang regarded Manchuria as the key ground. He decided to send his best troops to Manchuria and to control the big cities and main lines of communication in north and central China.

Superpower assistance

Chiang hoped that the United States would help him to carry out his grand strategic moves, but the American government was reluctant to give full support. Initially, US sea and air units were used to move *Kuomintang* troops into the cities of the eastern plains, but not into Manchuria itself, where Soviet troops and Mao's communists were present in force.

The United States still hoped for a compromise peace settlement, and all through the Civil War tried to restrain and influence Chiang by alternately refusing and providing assistance. All attempts to bring about a permanent ceasefire failed.

On the other side, the Soviets believed that Mao could not achieve victory because of the *Kuomintang*'s superiority of numbers and weaponry. Stalin hedged his bets; he maintained correct diplomatic relations with the *Kuomintang* and gave material help to the communists. Like President Harry Truman, Stalin was unable to restrain his clients; in 1948 he decided that the communists could win and gave them open support.

Communist strategy in the Civil War

When Japan surrendered, the communists were fully prepared to take action. Between August and October 1945 they expanded their area of control from 116 to 313 counties. Their policies of land reform and patriotic unification had a strong appeal to the peasants.

Mao's Red Army of experienced guerrillas was in good order; it was well disciplined, united, loyal, and indoctrinated. The command structure was simple. The Communist Party leaders worked out general principles and aims, leaving the local commanders to choose the best way of achieving them.

There was also a clear strategic plan; the newly formed Fourth Field Army would seize and attempt to hold Manchuria. The Second and Third Field Armies would act in north and central China to destroy roads and railways, and block the approach of *Kuomintang* troops from their base in the southwest. The aim of all operations was to be the destruction of enemy forces, not the control of ground.

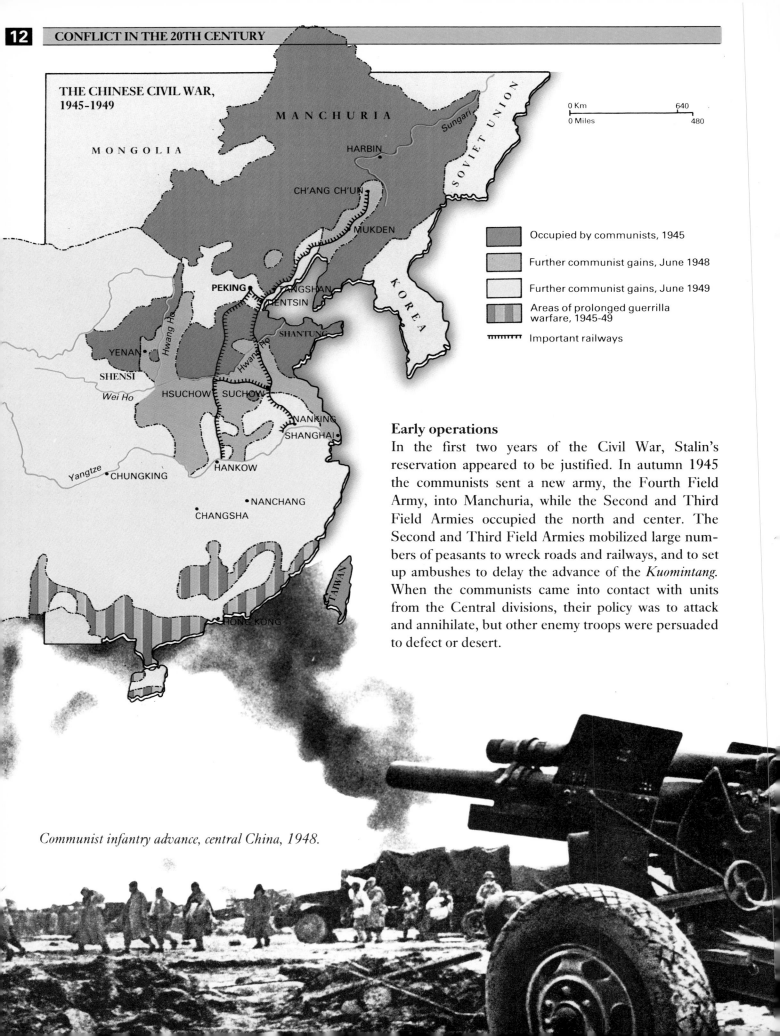

THE CHINESE CIVIL WAR, 1945–1949

MANCHURIA

MONGOLIA

SOVIET UNION

HARBIN

CH'ANG CH'UN

MUKDEN

KOREA

PEKING

TANGSHAN

TIENTSIN

SHANTUNG

YENAN

Hwang Ho

SHENSI

Hwang Ho

Wei Ho

HSUCHOW SUCHOW

NANKING

SHANGHAI

Yangtze CHUNGKING

HANKOW

NANCHANG

CHANGSHA

TAIWAN

HONG KONG

0 Km — 640
0 Miles — 480

Occupied by communists, 1945

Further communist gains, June 1948

Further communist gains, June 1949

Areas of prolonged guerrilla warfare, 1945–49

Important railways

Early operations

In the first two years of the Civil War, Stalin's reservation appeared to be justified. In autumn 1945 the communists sent a new army, the Fourth Field Army, into Manchuria, while the Second and Third Field Armies occupied the north and center. The Second and Third Field Armies mobilized large numbers of peasants to wreck roads and railways, and to set up ambushes to delay the advance of the *Kuomintang*. When the communists came into contact with units from the Central divisions, their policy was to attack and annihilate, but other enemy troops were persuaded to defect or desert.

Communist infantry advance, central China, 1948.

Despite these measures, the *Kuomintang* Army advanced through the coastal plain and up into Manchuria. The Red Army was forced to disperse into wilderness sanctuaries in Shantung and Shensi; in Manchuria the Fourth Field Army was driven out of the cities and went north to form a base beyond the Sungari River.

By spring 1946 the *Kuomintang* held all the great centers of population in China but it had not destroyed the communists and was unable to control the rural areas. Chiang was forced to hold the cities for reasons of prestige, and had to control the railways to link and supply his garrisons.

The communists gain the upper hand

In 1947, the balance of power began to shift. The *Kuomintang* Army was eroded by desertion, casualties and demobilization. The Red Army was growing, recruiting and training peasants, absorbing defectors. In the spring Chiang mounted a series of offensives intended to destroy the communists in Shantung and the northwest; his mobile columns gained ground, driving the communists from established sanctuaries, but they lacked the vigor to achieve complete success.

In the summer, when the *Kuomintang* thrusts were exhausted, the communists went over to the offensive, which had the desired effect of depriving the *Kuomintang* of reserves in Manchuria. In December, having spent a year in careful preparations, the Fourth Field Army launched a winter offensive in Manchuria.

By late spring 1948 the communists had their enemy imprisoned in the cities, deprived of intelligence and unable to maneuver. Strategic isolation was completed by the seizure of stretches of railway, particularly in areas south of Mukden and Ch'ang Ch'un. The *Kuomintang* response to the offensive was hesitant and sluggish. Attempts to relieve the isolated cities were thwarted by ambushes; the use of airlift to resupply Ch'ang Ch'un was ruinously expensive. One by one the demoralized garrisons were overrun, culminating in the fall of Mukden on November 2, 1948.

The communists' victory in Manchuria was a catastrophe for the *Kuomintang*. The communists gained the main industrial area of China, doubled the size of the Fourth Field Army, and were free to use it in north China. The *Kuomintang* had lost about 500,000 of their most reliable and best-equipped soldiers. Chiang lost prestige, and this had a devastating effect because the cohesion of the *Kuomintang* was based to a large extent on personal loyalty to him as a successful leader.

The defeat of the *Kuomintang*

The failure in Manchuria was compounded by defeat in the center of China, in a series of battles around Hsuchow, a vital point on the main railway network. In this struggle, the *Kuomintang* commanders had the advantage of superior equipment, but were outmaneuvered by their communist opponents. The last of the *Kuomintang* mechanized formations were destroyed by ambush. In the north, the communists were deploying to encircle garrisons in the area of Peking and Tientsin.

By late December 1948, Peking and Tientsin were in a pocket, and the communists (now operating under the title of the People's Liberation Army) began to reduce the cities one by one. In January 1949 full-scale assaults took Tangshan and then Tientsin. In some areas, the *Kuomintang* troops did not resist; in others they changed sides. In Peking the garrison commander gave up the city without a fight.

The fall of Peking led to confusion in the leadership of the *Kuomintang* and to the temporary eclipse of Chiang. However, his successor, Li Tsung-Jen, was unable to reach a satisfactory agreement with the communists. The war resumed and Chiang returned. But the *Kuomintang* Army lacked the will to fight. In April 1949 the communists started a general advance southward. The Yangtze River, the last great obstacle, was crossed virtually unopposed; Nanking and Shanghai fell without hard fighting.

Chiang gathered together his most loyal troops and as much treasure as he could and fled to the island of Taiwan (Formosa) to rest, recuperate, reform, and plan a return to the mainland. It never happened.

A communist China

On October 1, 1949, Mao proclaimed the foundation of the Chinese People's Republic. The victorious People's Liberation Army (PLA) paraded in triumph through Peking. On that day it ceased to be merely an insurrectionary force and became an instrument of state. This new role imposed traditional commitments, such as the defense of frontiers, recovery of lost territory, and intimidation of neighbors.

The discharge of these commitments was sometimes contrary to the Red Army's original role, that of vanguard of the communist revolution, servant and leader of the masses. It was a dilemma that was to cause problems as Mao's new government faced the reality of political power in a country weakened by revolution and war. The victory in 1949 was merely the beginning of a long and difficult road to recovery.

Mao Tse-tung (in jeep) inspects PLA tanks, 1949.

CHAPTER 2
CONSOLIDATING POWER

Since 1949, China has struggled to restore itself as the greatest Asian power. The process has not been easy. For 30 years, the first priority was security against internal and external enemies of the revolution, leading to military actions on the borders with North Korea, India, the Soviet Union and Vietnam. The role of the People's Liberation Army (PLA) changed, culminating in the Cultural Revolution of the late 1960s, when it assumed an unusual degree of political power. Mao Tse-tung then took steps to reassert himself but after his death in 1976 there was a power struggle. The new leadership, with the backing of the PLA, has concentrated on policies of modernization and industrialization, using the technology of the West. Once these succeed, China will achieve the power and influence befitting a country of its size, population and resources.

In autumn 1949 the leaders of the Chinese Communist Party were concerned above all else with security. Having taken power by force, they feared a violent counterattack on the revolutionary government by reactionaries. They also perceived a threat to the national territory of the Chinese People's Republic, and were determined to recover lost territory.

All around China there were threats to be countered and lands to be recovered, except along the frontiers with the Soviet Union. Here, China had territorial claims which were dropped, because of a sense of comradely solidarity coupled to a dependence on the Soviets for protection against the United States.

Traditionally, Chinese security policy regarded internal enemies as more dangerous than external enemies. The communists conformed to this view in 1949, and gave a high priority to the destruction of Chiang and his supporters. In rural areas the People's Militia conducted a ruthless purge of "class enemies" – reactionaries such as landowners, moneylenders and priests – and executed many *Kuomintang* supporters. Plans were made to "complete the revolution" by invading Taiwan and destroying the *Kuomintang* base.

The *Kuomintang* establishes itself in Taiwan

The *Kuomintang* controlled not only Taiwan itself, but other territories close to the mainland: the Tachen islets off Chekiang, the Pescadores scattered across the Taiwan Strait, the Quemoy group off Amoy, and the Matsu group off Foochow.

In late October 1949, the PLA attempted to improvise an amphibious assault on Quemoy. Due to a sudden change in the weather, this operation was a catastrophe. The PLA then began to make more detailed plans and preparations for an attack on Taiwan itself. In this they were encouraged by a firm belief, created by American statements, that the United States would not intervene to protect the *Kuomintang*.

The PLA assembled a force of 250,000 troops and 5,000 junks for the invasion of Taiwan, but it was never launched. On June 25, 1950 the North Koreans invaded South Korea, and, in response, on the 27th, the US Seventh Fleet arrived in the Taiwan Strait. The communist forces then prepared to defend the mainland against an invasion by the *Kuomintang*.

This stalemate has persisted ever since, despite the urgent desire of both Mao and Chiang to break it. The communists wished to invade Taiwan and wipe out a persistent source of opposition to the revolution, but lacked the maritime power to do this in the face of the US naval presence. The *Kuomintang* wanted to return to the mainland, but could not do so without US consent. The United States would not allow Chiang to attack the mainland in strength, but remained committed to defending Taiwan against attack.

The Quemoy crisis

The most violent crisis over Taiwan occurred in 1958, when the People's Republic applied a series of military, psychological and diplomatic measures to gain political advantage. Mao had a number of reasons for instigating this action. First, the balance of nuclear power had shifted in favor of the Soviet Union since 1954, which meant that the United States could no longer threaten nuclear strikes in defense of Taiwan, provided of course, that the Soviets were prepared to show comradely solidarity. Mao may have wished to test the quality of this solidarity. Second, he wished to remove the threat arising from the *Kuomintang* occupation of the offshore islands. This was especially important as there were plans to supply American missiles to Taiwan. Finally, a crisis might provide opportunities to put a strain on US-*Kuomintang* relations, and help to restrain or isolate Chiang.

The PLA applied two forms of pressure on the Quemoy group of islands; the navy attempted a seaborne blockade, while the army inflicted intense bombardments. Violent action continued throughout August and September, but died away in October. This was because the United States made it clear to both sides that it intended to maintain the *status quo*. The Soviets did nothing effective to support China.

Learning to live with the *Kuomintang*

The question of Taiwan continued to disturb Sino-American relations until the late 1960s, when the communists decided that countering the Soviet threat was more important than completing the revolution. The communists continued to maintain that Taiwan was part of China and must be reunited with the mainland. The United States accepted this view in 1972, but did not abandon the *Kuomintang* entirely.

The communist line moderated in the 1970s. The new policy was to woo Taiwan back to China with generous offers of a long and very gradual period of adjustment to the mainland political system. As yet, the *Kuomintang* leadership has resisted these invitations to "peaceful reorganization."

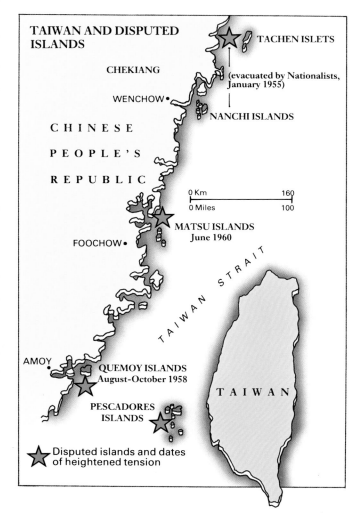

TAIWAN AND DISPUTED ISLANDS

TACHEN ISLETS

CHEKIANG

(evacuated by Nationalists, January 1955)

WENCHOW

NANCHI ISLANDS

CHINESE PEOPLE'S REPUBLIC

0 Km 160
0 Miles 100

MATSU ISLANDS
June 1960

FOOCHOW

TAIWAN STRAIT

AMOY

QUEMOY ISLANDS
August-October 1958

TAIWAN

PESCADORES ISLANDS

Disputed islands and dates of heightened tension

Regaining Tibet

The People's Republic had more success in dealing with Tibet, a country that had been part of the Chinese empire for centuries, but had gained more and more independence during the late 19th century. In 1916, encouraged by the prospects of help from British India, Tibet claimed complete independence.

But in 1949 China had a government determined to exercise control over all territory which had previously been part of the empire, and the British had left India in 1947. The government of India was anxious to remain on good terms with China. The communist leaders, therefore, decided to secure their southwest flank, and to bring the "benefits of socialism" to the Tibetans. The Tibetans had little military power, but proved very adept at passive (nonviolent) resistance to social change. They had a mystical and spiritual approach to life, which was inspired by the religious leader, the Dalai Lama, and found little appeal in the Chinese Communist Party's ideas or philosophy.

The military conquest of Tibet was easily accomplished. In autumn 1950 seven PLA divisions moved in, five advancing westward from Szechwan, two moving southwest from Sinkiang. This force of 35,000 marched to meet a Tibetan army of little more than 8,000, equipped with obsolete British weapons. There was only one significant action, when the Chinese forced a Tibetan position at Chamdo, on the road to the capital Lhasa, in a sudden, noisy night attack.

The Khamba nomad guerrillas in the eastern province of Kham were the only opposition encountered by the Chinese. But the conquest was not without its perils. The wild terrain, bleak climate and supply difficulties all imposed casualties.

By May 1951 the PLA had secured Lhasa, and the Tibetan government was forced to sign an "Agreement for Peaceful Liberation." The communists promised to respect the position of the Dalai Lama, guarantee freedom of religion and protect all religious institutions. The PLA then began to construct a network of military highways from China through Tibet, and to set up a communications system. For a few years, Tibetan society continued to function undisturbed.

Imposing communist ideas on Tibet

By 1954 the roads were complete, and the Chinese communists were in a radical mood, determined to extend their ideology into Tibet. They proceeded to try to destroy traditional Tibetan society by a series of actions which eventually provoked a national uprising in 1959.

The whole basis of the Tibetan way of life was religious. The Chinese attempted to discredit religion by propaganda in favor of modern science and technology, and communism. Practical benefits were demonstrated by the introduction of modern hospitals, motor transport, telephones and other facilities.

The next step was a wholesale reform of land law and taxation, to destroy the wealth and power of the nobility and monasteries, and to enrich the peasants, but these bribes did not attract the support of the Tibetan people. In their frustration, the Chinese decided that they must destroy the authority of the Dalai Lama and so divide the people. To do this, they used the Panchen Lama – a religious rival to the Dalai Lama – as an alternative focus of loyalty. None of these efforts was fully successful.

In 1956, the communists sent Chinese settlers to colonize eastern Tibet and to provide the basis for a local militia. This led to a fierce uprising by the Khambas, and the Chinese foreign minister, Chou En-lai, had to promise that the Chinese would moderate the pace of change in Tibet.

The flight of the Dalai Lama

This concession failed to produce tranquillity. The Khambas now believed that the only way to deal with the Chinese was by armed resistance, and this belief soon spread to Lhasa. By 1959 the atmosphere in the capital was tense. Eventually, the people of Lhasa, fearing that the Dalai Lama was about to be kidnapped, occupied the Summer Palace. Meanwhile, in the city there were violent demonstrations and attacks on Chinese soldiers.

The Dalai Lama could never approve of violence on his behalf, so he secretly left his palace and fled to India. The PLA then used artillery against Tibetans armed with nothing more than swords and stones, suppressing all rebellious activity with ruthless force. The government of Tibet was abolished and the country became an "Autonomous Region" (semi-independent province) of the People's Republic.

The containment of the Nationalists in Taiwan and the imposition of control over Tibet, although important to the internal security of the revolution in China, were only part of the problem facing the communist government in Peking in the 1950s. Of equal concern was the threat from outside powers, initially in Korea as the United States, under the banner of the United Nations, seemed intent on military action perilously close to the Chinese border.

THE KOREAN WAR

In 1945, having defeated the Japanese in Manchuria, the Soviets began to occupy the Korean peninsula, setting up a government based on the Korean Workers' Party led by Kim Il Sung. The United States hastily sent troops from the Army of Occupation in Japan to South Korea. The country was divided, supposedly on a temporary basis, until terms for unification could be agreed upon. North of the 38th parallel the North Koreans set up a communist state, with the backing of the Soviet Union. South of the parallel, the United States sponsored a government led by Syngman Rhee.

By 1950 North Korea had an army of nine strong divisions, equipped by the Soviets, and Kim Il Sung was ready for action. He was confident that he could invade and overrun the South. Statements from Washington had convinced him that the United States would not intervene, an impression reinforced by the communist victory in China in 1949. In any case, if the Americans decided to take military action, the Soviet Union and China would be obliged to assist North Korea and save Kim from defeat.

The Chinese were not as confident as Kim. Mao believed that the United States might be luring the North Koreans into making a move that the Western powers could use as an excuse for a full-scale atomic and conventional attack on the communist countries of Asia. But the Korean Workers' Party was much closer to the Soviet than the Chinese Communist Party, so Mao was unable to influence Kim.

The North Koreans launch their attack

On June 25, 1950 the North Korean People's Army surged across the 38th parallel in a surprise attack. The South Koreans, short of all essential material, were forced back. On June 29 the North Koreans took the South's capital, Seoul, and pushed on. But two days earlier the United Nations Security Council (which the Soviets had temporarily abandoned in protest against an American refusal to accept the Chinese People's Republic as the legitimate representative of China on the Council) had called on all UN members to help South Korea to defend itself.

On July 1, American troops began to arrive from Japan, and they set up a defense perimeter around Pusan, in the southeast corner of the peninsula. The North Koreans were stopped on this line. The United

THE KOREAN WAR, JUNE–SEPTEMBER 1950

➡ North Korean advances

▬ UN perimeter at Pusan, July 7

➡ UN landing at Inchon, September 15 and breakout from Pusan, September 19

States assembled substantial forces in Japan with a speed that the North Koreans had not considered possible. Other Western members of the United Nations sent contributions to the UN forces.

In the middle of September American marines landed on the west coast of Korea at Inchon, and advanced inland. Simultaneously, the forces in Pusan broke out and advanced north. This double blow completely disorganized the North Koreans, who streamed north in confusion. These developments were viewed with alarm in Peking. The communists were well aware that Korea had been the route taken by the Japanese to invade Manchuria in 1931.

A hostile presence in Korea would therefore be a direct threat to the heart of Chinese industry. The Chinese leadership accordingly sent messages to the United States, via India, that if the UN forces crossed the 38th parallel and approached the Yalu River along the northern border, China would feel threatened, and be forced to commit troops in a "forward defense."

The PLA had already reinforced the Fourth Field Army in Manchuria in the summer. Preparations for action were intensified, but were very effectively concealed. In fact, they were so well hidden that the US Administration refused to believe that China would act. The UN forces took Pyongyang, the capital of North Korea, on October 19, and pressed on. The PLA stealthily moved hundreds of thousands of troops (known as Chinese People's Volunteers) into North Korea. They moved only at night, and were not spotted by UN reconnaissance aircraft. By November the Chinese were in position to spring a major ambush on the UN forces.

The beachhead at Inchon, September 1950.

The Chinese involvement

On November 26, as the UN forces approached the Yalu, the Chinese emerged from the wilderness of the Taebaek Mountains, destroyed the South Korean II Corps, and forced the US Eighth Army into headlong retreat. They kept up the pressure by mass attacks at night, lying low under camouflage in daytime. Eventually they had to slow down, reduced by the superior firepower of the UN forces, and suffering from shortages of food and ammunition.

The UN forces made use of their motor transport to retreat farther, before consolidating south of the 38th parallel. Here they were hindered by North Korean guerrillas acting on the lines of communications.

On the other hand, the UN monopoly of effective airpower had less impact on the Chinese than had been expected. The latter absorbed huge casualties as a matter of routine, and were not dependent on vulnerable motor transport for their resupply. In January 1951 the Chinese and North Koreans renewed their attacks on the UN positions. They pushed 112 km (70 miles) south of the 38th parallel, but were yet again halted by supply difficulties.

CHINESE PEOPLE'S REPUBLIC

Yalu

Taebaek Mountains

Taedong

● WONSAN

● PYONGYANG

N O R T H   K O R E A

PANMUNJOM ——————— 38th Parallel

SEOUL
INCHON
Hangang

THE KOREAN WAR, NOVEMBER 1950-JULY 1953

S O U T H   K O R E A

PUSAN

0 Km   160
0 Miles   120

All through the war supply problems hampered the mobility of the Chinese. They could move fast on the battlefield, but their wider movements were sluggish, like those of a First World War European army. As soon as the Chinese were exhausted, the UN forces launched a succession of counteroffensives. These operations carefully coordinated the technically superior UN forces to destroy as many communist units as possible. By March 1951 the front line was roughly back on the 38th parallel.

At this stage the UN command was disturbed by conflicts of opinion over future strategy. The overall commander, General Douglas MacArthur, was keen to extend the war. He wanted to blockade the Chinese coast and to launch air raids on Manchuria, wrecking the Chinese armaments industry and demolishing bridges over the Yalu. He also proposed to put *Kuomintang* forces back into action on the mainland. These ideas were contrary to those of President Harry Truman, who wanted to limit the geographical extent of the war, avoid war with the People's Republic and end it with an honorable ceasefire. The conflict was resolved when Truman dismissed MacArthur.

UN advances up to November 24, 1950
UN raids toward Chinese border
Chinese advances launched November 26, 1950
Chinese advances up to January 24, 1951
UN counterattack, February-April 1951
UN advances up to March 31, 1951
Armistice line, July 27, 1953

US troops withdraw from PLA attack, 1950.

The Chinese fail

In April and May 1951 the Chinese made their final efforts to break through the UN lines, and failed. They had been reinforced, and supplied with heavy weapons from the Soviet Union, but it was not enough to match the firepower, mobility and flexibility of the UN forces. In particular, Chinese offensives were seriously disrupted by the UN forces' spoiling attacks. Their own maneuvers were too rigid to deal with unexpected setbacks and their massed infantry attacks were broken up by artillery or stopped on defensive lines. Those who got close to the UN positions were destroyed by machine guns. Casualties and failures weakened the morale of the Chinese soldiers. In late May 1951 the UN forces started to advance. By June whole battalions of the Chinese force were surrendering, whereas before hardly any prisoners had been taken.

Stalemate

Late in June 1951 the front stabilized, roughly along the line of the 38th parallel. Both sides dug deep positions. The Chinese mounted local attacks to try to improve their line, but made no further attempts to break through to the south. Between the lines a restless activity of costly patrols and raids went on, with control of no-man's-land or hilltops the objective.

This lasted for two years, until the summer of 1953. By then the Chinese communist leaders had decided that their army could not hope to defeat the UN forces, and were reassured that the UN would not attempt a direct attack on China. The Soviets, too, had lost interest in the war in Korea, especially after the death of Stalin (March 1953). On July 27, 1953 an armistice was concluded, which remains in force to this day.

Korea is still divided into two mutually hostile states. The United States maintains forces in the South; the Chinese and Soviets refuse to recognize the South and are committed to defend the North in the event of war. UN troops maintain an uneasy presence at Panmunjom, the scene of the armistice talks, but with large forces available to both the North and the South, Korea remains a "flashpoint" of considerable potential.

Nevertheless, the Korean War was a formative experience for the PLA, because for the first time it had been called upon to fight properly organized and equipped modern forces with competent commanders. These opponents forced the PLA commanders to recognize the weaknesses in their army. By 1953 the army had been reorganized, retrained and partially reequipped, chiefly along Soviet lines.

US troops in Korea

The US Army, drastically reduced in size since 1945, was still organized and equipped as if for the Second World War. Tanks such as the M4A3 Sherman and M24 Chaffee were already out of date. In the air, propeller-driven aircraft such as the F-51 Mustang fighter and B-26 Invader and B-29 Superfortress bombers made up the front-line forces.

As the war progressed, however, improvements were gradually introduced. On the ground, some new weapons appeared, notably uprated antitank rocket-launchers ("bazookas") and heavier tanks (such as the M26 Pershing), but the real changes came over tactics.

After June 1951, the Americans moved from a fluid infantry war to one of deliberate attrition, wearing down the enemy using massive firepower from artillery, tanks and ground-support aircraft. It was aptly termed "the meatgrinder" and it succeeded in preventing a communist breakthrough.

It was in the air that the major change occurred, for Korea was the first war in which jet-powered aircraft faced each other.

US air attack on North Korea, 1950.

As the North Koreans introduced Soviet-supplied MiG-15 jet fighters, the Americans responded with F-80C Shooting Stars and F-86A Sabres, producing battles for air supremacy over the North. Propeller-driven machines (especially bombers) continued to be used, but by 1953 a new era of air warfare had dawned.

Right: US heavy-mortar crew, 1952.

Below: The aftermath of battle, 1951.

BORDER DISPUTES

From 1949 until 1960 the People's Republic was friendly with the Soviet bloc, because of a mutual fear of the United States. From 1960 until 1968, however, China regarded both the United States and the Soviet Union as potential attackers, and since 1968 the People's Republic has tried to come to an arrangement with the United States to keep the Soviets in check. This became known as "ping-pong diplomacy;" started in 1969, it eventually led to formal recognition of the People's Republic by the United States in 1979.

The reasons behind the Sino-Soviet dispute were mainly ideological, but there were also territorial and strategic factors involved. The conflict emerged at two levels, between the communist parties on the one hand and the national governments on the other.

The ideological dispute sprang from the origins and experiences of the two communist parties. The Soviets gained power in 1917 by a *coup d'etat*, exploiting the discontent of urban workers. The Chinese revolution, however, had succeeded by building on a native tradition of peasant revolt.

By the mid-1950s these differences were becoming serious. This was partly because the Chinese no longer felt so insecure or in need of Soviet protection. Mao attempted to draw the Soviets into conflict with the United States during the 1958 Taiwan crisis. When the Soviets refused to become involved, he concluded that they were no longer true revolutionaries because they were unwilling to fight the "imperialists" (the Western powers). In 1960, the Chinese communist leadership publicly denounced the Soviet party, and a war of words has continued ever since.

Sino-Soviet rivalry

Once the Soviets were no longer regarded as comrades, the Chinese were free to pursue their territorial claims against the Soviet Union. These claims were primarily to territories annexed by the Russians before the 1917 Bolshevik revolution, and they were extensive. The Maritime Province of the Soviet Union, centered upon the port of Vladivostok and ceded to Russia in 1860, was the main area in dispute, followed by large areas along the frontiers of Manchuria and Sinkiang. The Chinese also disputed the status of Mongolia, nominally independent but a Soviet "satellite" (controlled territory) since 1921.

Indian transport problems in the Northeast Frontier Agency, 1962.

THE SINO-INDIAN WAR, 1962

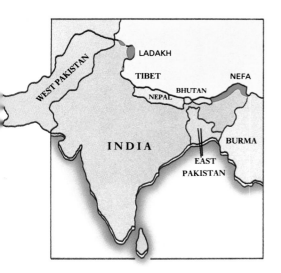

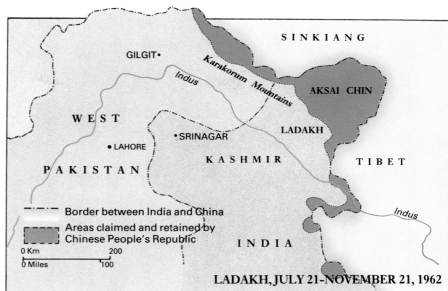

LADAKH, JULY 21–NOVEMBER 21, 1962

Legend:
- – · – · – Border between India and China
- Areas claimed and retained by Chinese People's Republic

0 Km — 200
0 Miles — 100

These Chinese claims were actively pursued from 1962 onward, and the former comrades in arms became bad neighbors. There have been innumerable violent incidents all along the 6,500-km (4,000-mile) frontier, notably in 1969 on the Ussuri River, where disputes over midstream islands led to fighting between rival forces. The Soviets continue to see the Chinese as a threat, although, in reality, the threat is very limited. China tested an atomic bomb in 1964, and a nuclear device in 1967, but has very small missile forces. The PLA is huge, but lacks the firepower and mobility essential for an effective attack on the Soviet Union, still depending primarily upon primitive railways for movement over long distances.

The invasion of Vietnam

China and the Soviet Union may be in stalemate on their border, but this has not prevented them from engaging in diplomacy and military action to gain influence in the rest of Asia. The Soviets and Chinese both supported the northern-based communists during the "National War of Liberation" in Vietnam. The Soviets established a predominant influence in Hanoi, the northern capital, and supported Vietnam in its expansion into Laos and Cambodia after 1975.

In an attempt to check the Vietnamese and to show support for China's allies in Kampuchea (Cambodia), the PLA was sent into northern Vietnam in spring 1979, attacking border towns in an effort to force a withdrawal of Vietnamese troops from Kampuchea. It enjoyed a degree of success – some Vietnamese units were redeployed and the PLA occupied key terrain –

but the Chinese withdrew as soon as it was felt that the objectives had been achieved. It showed how seriously the Chinese leaders viewed the threat.

The Sino-Indian Border Dispute

Similar fears have arisen over Soviet attempts to attract and retain the favor of India, leading in this case to a brief border war in 1962. The fighting took place in two separate areas of northern India – in the northwest among the barren mountains of Ladakh, close to Kashmir; in the northeast of India, in an area known as the Northeast Frontier Agency (NEFA). In the 1950s, the Chinese had been careful to maintain friendly relations with India, despite having frontier claims, but by 1960 the atmosphere had changed. India was critical of Chinese policy toward Tibet, while the Chinese regarded India as a willing tool of Soviet policies. It was a situation fraught with danger.

In Ladakh, the Indians had established a number of frontier posts in the Aksai Chin, a remote and rocky area that the Chinese considered to be rightfully theirs. From 1959 onward the PLA and the Indian Army deployed small posts as far forward as possible and ambushed each other's patrols.

The Chinese took this more seriously than the Indians, and in 1962 the PLA mounted an open attack. One by one the Indian outposts were eliminated by artillery fire and infantry assault. When the PLA finally stopped, it had gained all the territory claimed by China, improving its strategic access to Pakistan and Afghanistan as well as creating a barrier to direct Soviet contact with India.

The Northeast Frontier Agency

In the NEFA it was Indian complacency and frontier aggression that provided China with an excuse for action. In 1914, at a conference in Simla, British and Tibetan officials had agreed on what was known as the MacMahon Line as the northern border of India, and although no Chinese government had ever accepted this, it was respected by Peking.

The same was not the case with the Indians, however, for they interpreted Chinese policy as a sign of weakness. In the late 1950s, the Indian Army set up posts on the Chinese side of the Line, in an attempt to improve their hold on the frontier. The Indian government ignored Chinese protests, believing that a firm policy would guarantee success.

Fighting on the border

On October 9, 1962, the Indian Army in the western region of the NEFA tried to strengthen an advanced post at Dhola, below the Thag La ridge, by occupying a knoll at Tseng-Jong. The PLA pushed them off the knoll and then, on the night of October 19-20, launched a full-scale offensive, breaking through the Indian defenses in the area. The fighting soon revealed that the PLA was much stronger than its opponents. The Chinese troops were better clothed, equipped and trained to fight in the mountains and they were sustained by a good network of military roads. They also acted in accordance with a clear plan and had a simple command structure.

In contrast, many of the Indian soldiers were not acclimatized, clothed or equipped for the high places and their supply line soon failed. These handicaps were aggravated by political interference which prevented local commanders from acting as they saw fit. As a result, the PLA quickly advanced over the mountain passes in the NEFA and approached the plains beyond, destroying large portions of the Indian Army sent to oppose them. Then, on November 22, the Chinese declared a ceasefire and made partial withdrawals, announcing that their intention had been not to defeat the Indians (an event which could have triggered a Soviet response) but merely to "punish" them for border infringements. As they withdrew, however, the PLA made sure that they kept hold of the dominating ground along the frontier.

Present Sino-Indian relations

Since 1962, the Sino-Indian border has been relatively quiet, with only minor incidents occurring. The Indians, aware of the continued presence of Chinese troops in Tibet and of the influence of the PLA in remote tribal areas of the NEFA, where insurrection is always a threat, have accepted the settlement of 1962, but the Chinese still fear the consequences of possible Soviet gains in India.

This has been made worse by the fact that China's friendship with Pakistan in the 1960s (designed to counter Indian strength) was effectively undermined by the defeat of Pakistan in the war with India in 1971, and was not helped by the Soviet invasion and occupation of Afghanistan in 1979. This isolated Pakistan further and forced it into the American sphere of influence. This means that the borders of China would seem to be under constant threat. The Sino-Soviet dispute is far from over.

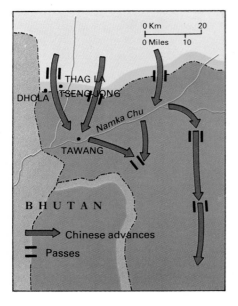

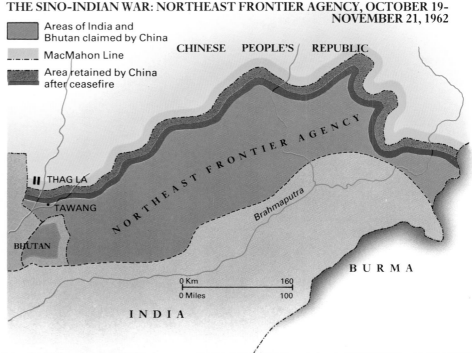

THE SINO-INDIAN WAR: NORTHEAST FRONTIER AGENCY, OCTOBER 19-NOVEMBER 21, 1962

Areas of India and Bhutan claimed by China

MacMahon Line

Area retained by China after ceasefire

THE PLA AND INTERNAL PROBLEMS

Such a history of fear and border clashes has inevitably affected the internal politics of communist China, particularly in terms of the role of the PLA. In Imperial China, official philosophy regarded military activity as abhorrent. In contrast, the Chinese Communist Party saw "armed class war" (the struggle of the peasants against their masters) as a means to transform society, and the Red Army as the spearhead of revolution.

According to Mao, there could be no progress without violence. The ruling class would not give up its power and wealth unless forced to do so. Therefore, "struggle" had a much wider meaning than the simple use of violence; indeed, a revolutionary movement could not succeed without the determination to employ force if necessary. Furthermore, according to Mao a fundamental change of attitude among the "oppressed classes of society" (the peasants and workers) and involvement in armed struggle would help to bring about this change.

The PLA's role

For these reasons the PLA has always been at the center of political life in the People's Republic, and the Chinese Communist Party has always been prepared to use force to deal with internal problems. The nature of the PLA itself has been a matter of violent controversy. The Maoist view was that the primary aim of the Communist Party was to create a wholly classless and unified society as quickly as possible. To that end, the PLA had to be closely integrated with society, the People's Militia (part-time, locally raised soldiers) had to be as extensive as possible so that "everyone was a soldier;" the soldiers had to do industrial and agricultural work; the main role of the army had to be internal; and the army had to prize loyalty to the revolution above military efficiency.

Less radical elements in the Communist Party, however, believed that the main role of the PLA was to defend the country against external enemies, notably the United States and Soviet Union. For this reason, the army had to be well equipped and intensively prepared for modern warfare, with emphasis on political training. In 1959 and again in 1965, the supporters of the Maoist view won political arguments over the nature of the army, and succeeded in keeping it "Red" rather than "Expert."

Dealing with internal threats

On becoming a national army in 1949, the PLA had to cope with internal threats to the People's Republic. These threats came from two sources: the non-Chinese minorities and "ideological dissidents" (opponents of the revolution).

The ethnic minorities numbered about 40 million (about 3.5 per cent of the population in the late 1940s), but many lived in thinly populated border areas. In particular, after the break with the Soviet Union in the 1960s, the Muslim nomads of Sinkiang and the Mongols of Inner Mongolia were seen as vulnerable to Soviet influence. The PLA dealt with this threat by providing medical and other services to the minorities, by recruiting considerable numbers of them, and by maintaining forces in the border areas.

In addition, vulnerable areas were colonized by Chinese settlers to form the basis for local militia units. When necessary, the PLA used massive force to crush rebellious minorities; in 1965, for example, a revolt in Sinkiang was put down.

In the 1950s the "ideological dissidents" consisted of political opponents (known collectively as "class enemies") and *Kuomintang* supporters. Many of the former were executed, driven into exile, or converted to communism. In the cities and in coastal or border areas, the People's Armed Police and Public Security Forces were responsible for dealing with all such opponents.

The Great Leap Forward

In the early 1950s, the Communist Party's main aims were to dispossess (confiscate the wealth of) landowners, moneylenders and capitalists, to give land to the peasants and to improve the living standards of industrial workers. Local militia, occasionally supported by PLA units, used force against "class enemies," but in the late 1950s the communist leadership decided it was time to go one stage further.

The aims of the subsequent "Great Leap Forward" were to abolish individual ownership of land and to place it in the hands of the peasants, organized into communist-controlled "collectives" or large farms; to transfer industry from the cities to villages; and to create a new system of government based on self-governing units known as autonomous communes. These aims encountered some opposition. Peasants were reluctant to give up their land or to work for a communist-dominated team rather than for the family. Moving industry from the towns was unpopular with the factory workers.

Chinese soldiers were sent out into the fields to help the peasants during the Cultural Revolution, 1971.

In areas where opposition was serious, the PLA was used to overcome it. However, some of the soldiers sympathized with the opposition, and the "Great Leap" was not a complete success. Important industrial concerns remained concentrated in the cities, and every peasant family was, in the end, allowed to retain a small plot of land for private use.

Mao was convinced that the PLA had lost its revolutionary zeal and was in need of reform. The Minister of Defense, Peng Te-Huai, was sacked, to be replaced in 1959 by Mao's disciple, Lin Piao. The political education of soldiers in the PLA was reformed, based on close study of Mao's *Little Red Book*.

By 1964, Mao felt the army was ready to lead the revolution again. Teams were sent into the countryside to spread revolutionary ideas. This was known as the "Socialist Education Movement" and was a build-up to the "Cultural Revolution," the greatest period of turmoil in China since 1949.

The Cultural Revolution

Mao believed that society was divided into the "Economic Base" – the masses of workers and peasants who produced material goods – and the "Cultural Superstructure," which consisted of intellectuals who provided the ordinary people with culture and political ideas. The role of the Communist Party, as the dominant force in the Superstructure, was to educate and lead the masses, but to do so with humility and respect for the collective wisdom of workers and peasants.

Mao's opponents in the Communist Party, however, believed that the masses were politically backward, and had to be driven on, if necessary by force, by the Party leadership. By the mid-1960s Mao believed that the Party had become arrogant, complacent and lazy.

The aim of the "Great Proletarian Cultural Revolution" was to destroy the elite nature of the Superstructure, and force it to accept the ideas of the Base. Radical school and university students were to stir up the masses to criticize the Superstructure. This process started in 1966. Initially, the PLA was only involved to the extent of advising the students and providing essential supplies.

As the struggle developed, the Superstructure proved more resistant to change than anticipated. The students formed Red Guards, raised mass organizations from within the Base, and began to use force. Some PLA regular units tried to protect local Communist Party and government officials from the radicals, but were ordered not to do so by Mao.

He wanted the Cultural Revolution to succeed, even if it meant some disorder. In 1967 the mass organizations began seizing power from local officials. The Red Guards were ordered to return to school and university, but many refused to do so. The PLA then had to round them up and send them home.

The PLA takes over

In the summer of 1967 some senior PLA commanders expressed alarm at the extent of the disorders. They felt that the virtual collapse of Party and government authority might tempt the United States or the Soviet Union to attack China.

From autumn 1967, the PLA began to set up new organizations to take control of areas where government had been destroyed. A network of revolutionary committees was set up, dominated by the army. In spring 1969, the unrest died down, leaving the PLA effectively in control. Lin Piao was appointed Vice-Chairman of the Communist Party and China came under military rule.

At once, Mao began a struggle to reestablish control of the Communist Party and to reassert his leadership. In 1971 Lin died, along with his closest supporters, in a plane crash in Mongolia. Two years later, a major reshuffle of senior army commanders proved that the PLA was under political control again.

When Mao died in 1976, however, it was the attitude of the majority of the PLA's senior commanders that ensured that Mao's widow, Chiang Ching – the leader of the "Gang of Four" – was unable to seize power. Indeed, when the leadership struggle was finally resolved in 1982, it was the PLA's chief of staff, Teng Hsiao-ping (a victim of radical criticism during the Cultural Revolution), who emerged victorious.

New directions

The promotion of Teng heralded a period of change in China which is still being played out. Since 1982 the country has adopted a much less radical stance in domestic and world affairs. This is aimed at building up China's economic strength.

In order to modernize its industry, however, the Chinese leadership has had to alter its foreign policy, toning down its opposition to countries which may be of help. As early as 1978, for example, a commercial agreement was signed with Japan, the traditional enemy. This coincided with approaches toward the United States, partly to gain access to the new technology of the West but also as a means of further isolating both Taiwan and the Soviet Union, still viewed as potential opponents.

Teng's pursuit of Western technology and his new relations with the Western powers has begun to achieve results, not least in the agreement with Britain over the future of Hong Kong, one of the last of the European-controlled coastal enclaves which had caused so much aggravation in the past. It seems that once the Chinese regain control of Hong Kong in 1997, it will be retained as a center of world trade and commerce.

It is a compromise as far as the communism of the revolution is concerned, but it may ensure that, in the future, China becomes the great power which her size, population and resources always promised.

Chinese heavy industry: production at the iron and steel works at Wuhan was severely disrupted during the Cultural Revolution. In the 1970s the plant was modernized with the help of Western experts.

The Japanese surrender, September 1945.

CHAPTER 3

JAPANESE RECONSTRUCTION

From 1900 until the mid-1940s, Japan was strong in military and naval terms. Policies of conquest resulted in Japanese domination of large areas of Southeast Asia, China and the Pacific, but Allied victory in 1945 led to American occupation of Japan. Yet Japan recovered, concentrating on industrial strength as a new source of power and influence while sheltering behind the United States for defense. This produced strains. Economic revival led to intense competition with other industrialized countries, and new American moves in the 1970s left Japan unsure of the future. By the 1980s, however, Japan seemed poised to resume its role as one of the "great powers" of the modern world.

The islands of Japan – principally Hokkaido, Honshu, Shikoku and Kyushu – cover a land area of some 370,000 square km (143,000 square miles) and are situated off the east coast of the Asian landmass. They contain few deposits of the raw materials needed to create industrial wealth – there is no oil, aluminum or nickel and very little coal, iron ore or copper – and cannot produce enough food to supply a growing population (currently 122 million). Yet Japan has dominated the affairs of Asia and the Pacific for much of the 20th century and, by virtue of industrial expertise, continues to occupy a key position in world as well as regional economic life.

Japanese society

This is a remarkable achievement for a country the size of Japan, made more so when it is remembered that 150 years ago few people in Europe or America had even heard of Japan, let alone penetrated its borders to study its social or political framework. If they had, they would have found a country containing an Emperor whose position was that of a god and, more significantly, one that was ruled by a privileged class of landowners *(Daimyo)* who maintained their power through armed warriors known as *Samurai*.

These warriors had helped to create a very rigid society, based on a militaristic code of honor (*Bushido*) which allowed them to dictate the policies of government. Since the 16th century, the *Samurai* had insisted on seclusion from outside powers, viewing all foreigners as agents of change which would disrupt the ordered nature of Japanese society.

But this was not an attitude that could last indefinitely. By the 1850s, as American and then European traders began to explore the potential of the Pacific, Japan had been forced to face reality, particularly when it was discovered that the strangers were backed by weapons that the *Samurai* could not defeat. When this coincided with a realization that the home islands could no longer produce the food and materials needed by the population, Japan had no choice but to open itself to the world.

In the process, however, the Japanese leadership was anxious to avoid the exploitation that usually accompanied Western trade. Observing the fate of China, the Japanese decided to absorb the advantages of new technology while retaining the old ways. By the late 19th century, Japan had a powerful navy, capable of controlling the sea-lanes around the home islands, and a mass army strong enough to seize the sources of raw material so essential to economic growth.

Japanese expansion
As Japanese forces fought successful wars against China (1894-95) and, more significantly, Russia (1904-05), the twin pressures of militarism and nationalism combined to produce a strong movement dedicated to prosperity through conquest. They also ensured that the armed forces were able to dominate civilian politicians.

By the late 1930s, this movement in favor of conquest had led to a Japanese seizure of Korea (in 1910) and to attacks on Manchuria (1931) and China (1937). But wars are expensive, requiring an industrial strength that could not be guaranteed in islands so short of raw materials, and it is against this background that the Japanese decision to attack the European and American possessions in Southeast Asia and the Pacific in December 1941 must be seen.

The primary aim was to create a "Greater East Asia Co-prosperity Sphere," incorporating the Philippines, Malaya, Borneo and the Dutch East Indies (Indonesia), which would be under the exclusive control of Japan, releasing the raw materials needed to feed an insatiable war machine. Despite civilian opposition to such an ambitious move, military and naval leaders went ahead, hoping to establish a position of such strength that the Europeans and Americans would be deterred from attacking it.

Japanese defeat
Unfortunately for the Japanese, this did not happen. The Allies mounted counteroffensives that gradually recovered lost ground. As the Japanese fleet was ground down in successive battles in the Pacific, the way was opened for Allied attacks which, by 1945, had penetrated as far as Iwo Jima and Okinawa, close to the main islands of Japan.

By then, a combination of submarines, sea-mines and aircraft had virtually destroyed the Japanese merchant shipping fleet, effectively starving the country of raw materials. A bombing campaign, mounted initially from China and then from the Mariana Islands in the central Pacific, had also devastated many of Japan's major cities. The bombing came to a climax in early August 1945 with the dropping of atomic bombs on Hiroshima and Nagasaki, and when this coincided with a Soviet invasion of Manchuria, the Emperor, normally uninvolved in government policy, had no choice but to order his forces to surrender.

Postwar Japan
Such a catastrophe undermined many of the traditional attitudes of the Japanese people and destroyed the existing social and political framework of the country. The armed forces were discredited and the policies of conquest widely blamed for creating the disaster of 1945, opinions which soon led to a determination among the Japanese people not to use armed force in the future.

This was reinforced by the policy of the United States as its army occupied the Japanese islands; Japan was to be totally and permanently disarmed, then reformed and restructured according to the principles of "liberal democracy." In 1946, as part of this process, the Americans devised and imposed a new Constitution which renounced war as an instrument of Japanese policy in the future and stated that Japan would no longer retain armed forces.

In case of threats to the country, Japan would rely on the United Nations and the United States for protection. At the same time, the role of the Emperor was altered from god to constitutional monarch, multiparty democratic elections were held and Japanese society was "purged" of all remnants of a militaristic past.

With American financial help, Japanese industry was rebuilt along peaceful lines, producing the first of the consumer goods which the rest of the world demanded. Recognizing the success of their postwar policies, the Americans quickly drew up a peace treaty which would welcome Japan back as a Western ally. In September 1951, Japan signed a security treaty with the United States, requesting the commitment of American forces to the defense of Japan, and this enabled the Americans to end their occupation a few months later. It also accepted the loss of territory suffered during the Second World War.

By then, the Korean War had altered the situation in Asia, introducing to the area all the pressures of rivalry between the United States and the Soviet Union. This undoubtedly benefited Japan, boosting the process of economic recovery and ensuring continued American interest in islands used as a base for the United Nations forces fighting in Korea.

Setting up the Self Defense Forces

It also created new pressures, undermining the pacifist trend of the immediate postwar years. In 1954, suddenly aware that the commitment to maintain armed forces permanently in Japan would be expensive, the American government put pressure on the authorities in Tokyo to form the Japan Defense Agency and to use the Police Reserve as the basis for Self Defense Forces.

The Self Defense Forces are unlike other armed forces. In 1957, the National Defense Council announced a basic policy for the forces. This specified that there would be no compulsory service, that the forces would not be deployed overseas, and that they would never have "weapons of aggression" such as long-range bombers. The policy also banned the production or presence of nuclear weapons.

The size of the forces has been limited by the numbers of men who are willing to serve, in a country where military affairs are unfashionable. Also there is an unofficial agreement that Japan should not spend more than one per cent of the annual gross national product (the amount of money "earned" by the country). In spite of all these limitations, the formation of the Self Defense Forces was highly controversial.

Relations with the United States

Nevertheless, the Self Defense Forces have never been regarded as capable of defending Japan on their own; they are merely a contribution, dependent in the end on the power of the United States. By the terms of the Security Treaty of 1951 (renewed in 1960 and 1972), the United States guarantees to protect Japan against aggression and, in return, is allowed to maintain military and naval bases on Japanese soil, as part of Washington's global response to the threat of communism.

To many Japanese, this threat is a very real one as both China and the Soviet Union occupy territory close to Japan itself or have forces capable of controlling sea-lanes essential to the survival of Japan. Soviet forces, using Vladivostok as a base, could mount air attacks on Japan, attempt to blockade the coast or cut the sea-lanes to Southeast Asia and beyond.

By the 1970s it was estimated that Japan needed access to 10 per cent of the world's exports and 10 per cent of its oil production just to survive, all of which would have to come in by sea. In such circumstances, the role of the United States is crucial, protecting the Japanese islands from invasion.

Antitank jeeps of Japan's Self Defense Forces.

Such a dependence upon the United States implies a need for both countries to view the world in much the same way. During the 1950s and 1960s, when Washington took the straightforward view that communism was on the march and had to be stopped, regardless of its source, this was not likely to cause problems, but in the 1970s the situation began to change. The United States decided to improve relations with Japan's traditional enemy, China, thus threatening the Soviet Union with encirclement. This was known as the "China card" in US-Soviet relations.

By 1973, with the withdrawal of US troops from Vietnam and the failure of the war to "contain" communism, it seemed as if Japan had no choice but to look to her own defenses far more. The crisis of 1973-74, when Arab oil-producing countries threatened to cut off supplies to states like Japan who were associated with the United States' support of Israel, did little to ease the situation.

Changing attitudes

These changes have been reflected in new Japanese attitudes to both defense and foreign affairs. As early as 1976, the Japanese government announced that it had authorized a build-up of air defense and anti-submarine warfare forces. This coincided with a more independent line in Japanese foreign policy, designed not so much to replace as to ease the dependence upon the United States.

However, Japan cannot afford to move too far away from the policies of the United States, and since the 1970s she has tended to reflect the changes imposed by Washington. By the end of that decade, for example, the Japanese had improved their relations with China, resuming diplomatic contact with Peking and gradually reducing their markets in Taiwan. It is now widely accepted that a combination of Japanese expertise and Chinese resources could produce an Asian economic bloc of enormous potential in the near future.

The Soviet threat

At the same time, the threat from the Soviet Union has not declined – indeed, the new relationship with China probably makes it worse – and the need for American long-term protection remains essential. Territorial disputes between Japan and the Soviet Union, particularly over the southern Kurile Islands and southern Sakhalin, which many Japanese refuse to recognize as Soviet possessions, have led to bitter clashes between Japanese fishermen and Soviet naval patrols. The

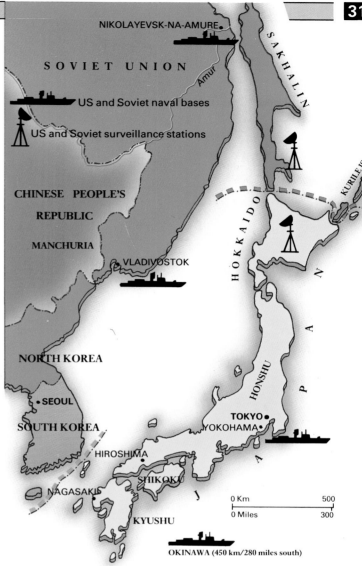

continued build-up of Soviet forces around Vladivostok has done nothing to ease the tension.

The Japanese continue to fear the power and intentions of the Soviet Union, particularly since Korean Air Lines flight 007 was shot down over Sakhalin by Soviet fighters on September 1, 1983. No one denies that the aircraft strayed into controlled Soviet airspace, but the ruthless Soviet response, leading to the death of 269 passengers and crew, shocked the world and acted as a reminder to the Japanese that they faced a formidable rival in east Asia. To the Soviets, it was a clear case of a "civilian" airliner being used to test the defenses of a sensitive area; to most other people it was an example of Soviet aggression.

There can be no doubt that Japan continues to occupy a vulnerable position in the confrontation between East and West and that her future security depends upon her relationship with the United States. But there are signs that Japan is now prepared to take a much more independent position in world affairs.

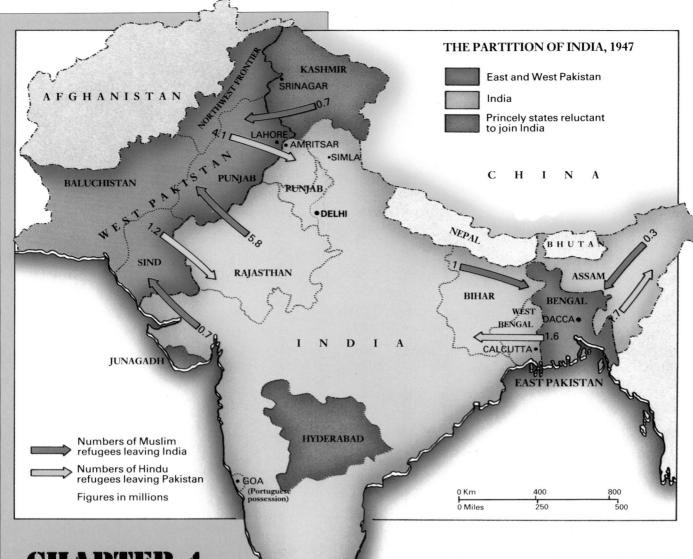

THE PARTITION OF INDIA, 1947

- East and West Pakistan
- India
- Princely states reluctant to join India

Numbers of Muslim refugees leaving India
Numbers of Hindu refugees leaving Pakistan
Figures in millions

CHAPTER 4

THE FRAGMENTED SUBCONTINENT

The Indian subcontinent, containing the countries of India, Pakistan and Bangladesh, as well as the off-shore island of Sri Lanka (Ceylon), has many problems. Split along religious lines when the British withdrew in 1947-48, it has been deeply affected by conflicts over territory, especially in Kashmir, and continues to experience trouble from internal factions fighting for political or religious beliefs. The problems are likely to persist.

In the 11th century, Muslims invaded India from the northwest, won successive victories over their Hindu opponents, and by the 16th century had established the Mughal Empire as the most powerful state in the subcontinent. In the 18th century Britain emerged as predominant after a series of wars against other European and native enemies. In the 19th century British reformers introduced liberal and scientific education to India. This created an educated middle class, which became democratic and nationalist in outlook.

A revival of Hinduism, hostile to Muslims and Christian missionaries, reinforced the middle-class nationalists and provided them with followers among the masses. Religious, cultural and political feeling combined to produce an independence movement.

From 1905 until 1947, Indian politics was dominated by two movements for independence. The Indian National Congress was set up in 1885 as an all-India party. It was led by intellectuals, influenced by socialist ideas, and assumed leadership of the Hindus, although there were some prominent Muslims involved. The Muslim League, set up in 1906, attracted support from the Muslim minority who regarded Congress as a primarily Hindu organization, and dreaded the prospect of a centralized state ruled by a Hindu majority.

Another important force in Indian politics was the Indian princes, who ruled 562 states of various sizes. They all had individual agreements with the British to define their status, and did not want to be absorbed into a democratic republic. The British authorities were faced with increasing agitation for self-government, and the impossible task of reconciling all these conflicting demands.

There were other groups clamoring for a say in India's future. The Sikhs, a sect of reformed Hindus, were small in number, but commanded respect for their dedication, organization and military prowess. The Bengalis, Muslim and Hindu alike, were numerous and productive, and at times ignored their religious differences. In fact, they had more in common with each other than with co-religionists from other parts of India.

Moves toward independence

The approach to independence was slow and difficult. During the First World War, the British government came under intensified pressure. The Americans had announced that the principle of national self-determination – self-government by peoples identified as nations – would be used as a guide to the settlement of postwar Europe. Congress eagerly took this up. In 1916 the Muslim League allied itself to Congress in the Lucknow Pact. The League was attracted by Congress assurances that when India was independent an electoral system would be devised to protect Muslims. It was also influenced by the fact that Britain was at war with Turkey, the foremost Muslim power.

The splendor of 19th-century India: the Maharaja of Kashmir and his court officials.

In 1917 Britain promised that India should progress to full self-government, but did not say when this would be achieved. From then on, having agreed on the principle of independence, the main issues concerned when and how it should be achieved.

Between the world wars the principle of "Dyarchy" (joint rule between the British and the Indians) was used to transfer increasing amounts of power to the Indian population. Dyarchy was applied to local politics in 1929, and to national government by 1935. But by then the population was no longer united.

As its support grew, pressure from Hindu extremists had led Congress to repudiate the scheme for an electoral system to protect the Muslims in 1927. This was seen as a betrayal and a threat by the League, and it provoked rioting between the religious communities. By 1937 the League had taken up the idea of a separate Muslim state, first conceived in 1930, and called for a partition or division of the country along religious lines.

By the time of the Second World War it was clear that Congress and the League could not be reconciled. Congress demanded independence, and wanted India to be a secular, centralized, democratic republic. The League did not regard Congress as secular, and repudiated the idea of a secular state anyway.

To Muslims, government by unbelievers, particularly by Hindus who worship many gods and venerate idols, would be intolerable. The League was prepared to contemplate an India organized as a loose confederation, with autonomy (or self-government) for its provinces and little power at the center of government.

During the war, the Muslims gave loyal support to the British, hoping for protection from the Hindus. Congress, however, refused to cooperate with the war effort and agitated for the British to "quit India." Some nationalists went further, and collaborated with the Japanese, who formed an Indian National Army (INA) of deserters and prisoners of war. Their action added bitterness to the struggle for independence.

The path to independence

In 1945 there were elections in which the 250 million Hindus and 90 million Muslims voted along predictable lines. The Congress won eight provinces, the League won three. The British were anxious to be free of commitments in India. Indications that British power was fading encouraged outbreaks of violence. In particular, the lenient treatment of the leaders of the Indian National Army provoked nationalist outrage and gave an impression of weakness.

In summer 1946 a British cabinet mission drew up plans for the transition to independence. These entailed the creation of an Interim Government and a Constitutional Assembly. The Interim Government was set up in September, with Pandit Jawaharlal Nehru, leader of the Congress, as leader.

Initially the League leaders refused to take office in this government. They changed their minds in October, but followed a policy of non-cooperation with the Congress ministers. However, they refused to enter the Constitutional Assembly, which had a Congress majority, because to do so might be seen as an acceptance of the principle of "One India." The League had demonstrated its power by calling for demonstrations. On August 16 a day of "direct action" in Calcutta led to three days of disorder. Muslims attacked Hindus; Hindus and Sikhs retaliated against Muslims. Some 100,000 families were burned out of their homes. In October massacres of Muslims took place in Bihar and Bengal. The army and police attempted to restrain the violence, but they were not strong enough. All over India mobs went on the rampage.

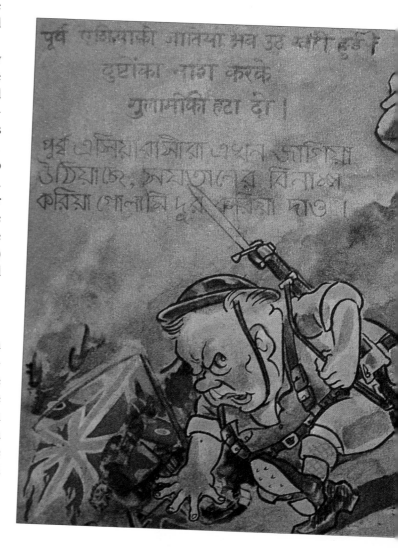

In spring 1947 Congress called on the British to force the League to participate in the Constitutional Assembly, or expel them from the Interim Government. It was obvious that the League and Congress could not cooperate, or even coexist.

But Congress and the British government were desperate to proceed to independence swiftly. In February the British prime minister, Clement Attlee, announced that India would be independent by June 1948, hoping that this prospect would persuade the League and the Congress to reach a settlement. The British decided that partition was inevitable and in June 1947 the government announced that India would be granted independence as two sovereign states, India and Pakistan, in August.

The Indian princely states were abandoned. Britain did not honor its commitments to protect them. By August 1947, all but three – Hyderabad, Junagadh and Kashmir – had accepted absorption. What happened to the three that attempted to claim independence was of political importance, particularly to relations between India and Pakistan.

An anti-British cartoon, 1942.

The problems of independence

The process of partition was controversial, difficult, and violent. It resolved a major issue, but gave rise to a host of new ones. Many Congress supporters refused to accept partition as legitimate, and regarded the very existence of Pakistan as absurd. The definition of the frontiers was difficult, producing long-term problems.

Violence led to enormous migrations of refugees, and the welfare of these people, and disposal of the property they had abandoned in terror, was a source of suspicion and hostility. The control of water resources was a troublesome question, as many great rivers, vital to agriculture, crossed the frontiers. The Indus River, which gave India its name, starts in the Himalayas and then flows through Pakistan. The Indians cut off the water supplies to Pakistan in the 1950s and this dispute was eventually settled by treaty in 1960. The sharing of resources of money, military formations, and material gave ample opportunity for accusations of dishonesty.

Pakistan emerged as three whole provinces of British India: Baluchistan, Sind and the Northwest Frontier Province, plus portions of three others, Punjab, Bengal and Assam. The "internal partitions" of Punjab and Bengal were particularly tragic in their effects.

Punjab and Bengal

The situation in Punjab was complicated by the presence of six million Sikhs who were determined to keep their traditional lands and holy places intact and undivided, and not to accept Muslim rule. As a result of their resolution, the district of Guradaspir, which had a majority of Muslims but also contained Amritsar, the Sikh holy city, was awarded to India by the Boundary Commission. This decision was regarded as outrageous by the Muslims.

The Sikhs set about consolidating their position by driving Muslims out of eastern Punjab. In the rural areas of west Punjab, Muslims retaliated against Sikhs and Hindus. As the British forces had withdrawn, and this Interim Government's mixed Border Force was paralyzed by internal arguments, massacres and huge movements of refugees continued unchecked.

The division of Bengal and Assam greatly injured the Bengali sense of cultural identity, and cut off producers of jute and tea in Pakistan from their traditional processors and markets in India. As in Punjab, the partition was accompanied by violence and mass migrations. It is estimated that in the process of partition 500,000 were killed and 14 million refugees were driven from their homes.

Relations between India and Pakistan

After independence, relations between India and Pakistan were bad. Each state felt threatened by the other. Indians feared the Muslims both as the ancient rulers of India and for their religious expansionism and warlike outlook. Pakistanis feared India; they were outnumbered and vulnerable because they were divided into an east and west wing. Also the Indian people clearly did not believe that Pakistan had any right to exist.

Both countries struggled to obtain security for themselves by gaining advantage over the other, using political, psychological, diplomatic, economic and military means. In both countries internal politics were dominated by highly emotional attitudes toward the other, and successive governments had to base official policy on these feelings.

Junagadh and Hyderabad

Pakistan's sense of insecurity was aggravated soon after independence by the Indian drive for national unity; in particular the use of force to absorb the princely states of Hyderabad and Junagadh. During the approach to independence the British had given the rulers of the states the right to join India or Pakistan, or to remain independent. However, Congress stated in June 1947 that for the sake of unity the states must accept absorption and democracy. By Independence all but three of the 562 states had opted for India or Pakistan.

In Junagadh the ruler, the "Nawab," was Muslim, but a large majority of the people were Hindus, and the state was surrounded by Indian territory. With the encouragement of the League, the Nawab opted for inclusion in Pakistan. He was not allowed to exercise his option. Indian troops massed on the frontiers, Hindu agitators stirred up disorder, and the state became ungovernable. In October 1947 the Nawab fled to Pakistan and the Indian Army moved in to restore order and install a provisional government that had been set up in advance.

Hyderabad also had a Muslim ruler, the "Nizam," and a predominantly Hindu population. The Nizam decided he wished to maintain full independence for his state. The Indian government concluded a "standstill agreement" with the Nizam in November 1947. But it was impossible for Hyderabad to survive. The state was landlocked in Indian territory, and was subjected to economic blockade. By September 1948 the Hindus and Muslims were fighting each other and the Indian Army moved in to occupy the state.

Pakistani fears

The Pakistanis drew two conclusions from the cases of Junagadh and Hyderabad. One was that the Indian government would not respect the principle of self-determination if it inconvenienced Indian national interests. The other was that despite its protestations of a nonviolent and antimilitary outlook, India was an aggressive and expansionist power.

They were afraid that Pakistan might be treated in the same way as Junagadh and Hyderabad. They were extremely conscious of their strategic vulnerability. Pakistan was in two wings separated by over 1,500 km (1,000 miles) of Indian territory. The Eastern wing was surrounded by India on three sides. The Western wing had a long vulnerable frontier in Punjab and Sind, with important political centers and strategic lines of communication uncomfortably close to India.

Because of these conditions, Pakistan was a struggling military state, with the army seen as the only effective means to ensure survival, and as the principal unifying force in the nation. The army assumed an important role in national politics, always ready to intervene in civil affairs. The emergence of the militaristic mentality in Pakistan confirmed Indian suspicions that her neighbor was dangerous and must be deterred from military adventures by the presence of superior forces. In this way, suspicions kept the level of tension high and led to a ruinous arms race, and to three wars between the two countries.

The Kashmir question

The first of these wars was fought between October 1947 and January 1949 over Kashmir. The status and control of Kashmir has been and remains the most obvious and important of the concrete issues causing hostility between India and Pakistan. In 1947 Kashmir had a Hindu Maharaja, Sir Hari Singh, and a population which was predominantly Muslim. The League had always regarded Kashmir as Muslim territory, and believed that Pakistan could not be whole without it.

The Maharaja did not wish to opt for Pakistan, or to offend the population by joining India. The people of Kashmir would have preferred independence or autonomy within a loosely organized state. The Indian government regarded control of Kashmir, particularly the strategic northern areas, as vital to Indian security. In July 1947 there was an uprising by Muslim peasants in Poonch, in the west of Kashmir. The Maharaja's army began to suppress the rebellion with enthusiasm.

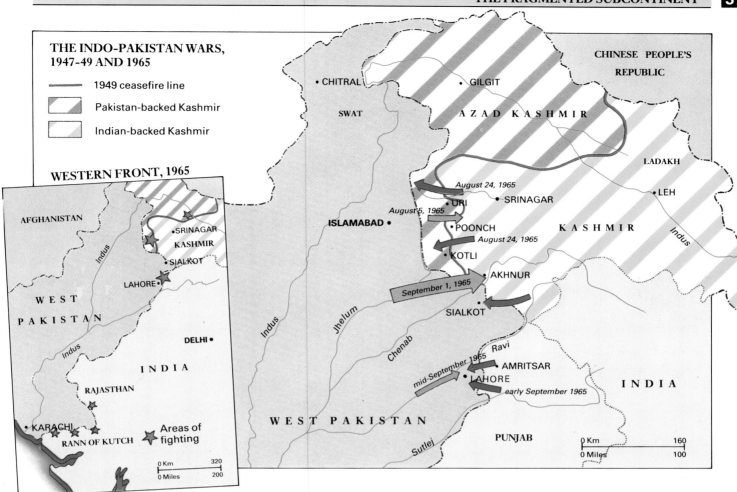

THE INDO-PAKISTAN WARS,
1947-49 AND 1965

- 1949 ceasefire line
- Pakistan-backed Kashmir
- Indian-backed Kashmir

WESTERN FRONT, 1965

Areas of fighting

In October, inspired by reports of massacres of Muslims, bands of warriors from the Northwest Frontier province invaded Kashmir. The Maharaja's army was thrust aside, and the tribesmen advanced on Srinagar, the capital. The Maharaja was forced to agree to join Kashmir to India as the price of help from the Indian Army. Indian troops were airlifted into Srinagar just before the Muslim irregulars arrived, and pushed them back eastward.

The Indian Government rejected the Pakistani proposal for a vote on the future of Kashmir because the Maharaja had opted for India, and this was held to be legally binding. In November the fighting spread; the Muslim hillmen of the northern regions of Gilgit, Swat and Chitral drove out the Maharaja's Hindu garrisons and declared for Pakistan. The Indian Army pressed on eastward until stopped by the onset of winter. Early in 1948 the Pakistani Army went to the aid of the tribesmen, and enforced a stalemate on the line Kotli-Poonch-Uri. Occasional fighting, patrol clashes, exchanges of artillery fire and minor attacks continued until the winter.

A temporary truce

On December 31, 1948 the Indian and Pakistani Chiefs of Staff concluded a truce which confirmed the military *status quo*. The United Nations sent out an observer force to patrol the ceasefire line and monitor the situation; the United Nations also proposed that the people of Kashmir should have a vote on whether to join India or Pakistan.

This was highly embarrassing for India, because Nehru based his foreign policy on neutralism, and was committed to using the United Nations; but he was also unable to contemplate losing Kashmir. The Indian people would be outraged if the government gave up Kashmir to Pakistan.

India demanded that the Muslim forces in Azad ("Free") Kashmir, under Pakistani protection, be disbanded, and the state reunited under the leadership of Sheikh Abdullah. Abdullah was a popular, nationalistic leader who was, for the moment, on excellent terms with Nehru. The Pakistanis refused Nehru's terms. The ceasefire left India in indirect control of most of Kashmir, with a population of 3.5 million. Azad Kashmir had a population of 700,000.

Sheikh Abdullah, leader of Kashmir

In the early 1950s Abdullah showed signs of wanting to make Kashmir more independent of India. In 1952 the Maharaja was forced out of the state, and Abdullah, as prime minister, was virtually dictator. In 1953 the Indian Occupation Forces arrested Abdullah and installed a local politician, who was easier to control, in his place.

It became obvious that India intended to absorb Kashmir, step by step, no matter how the Pakistanis protested or what the United Nations resolved. In 1954 Nehru declared that Kashmir was permanently part of India, and in 1957 that it was constitutionally part of the Indian Union.

Pakistan seeks allies

Pakistan looked for support to the Muslim countries, and to the Western powers. This was to counterbalance the historically close relationship between the Russian communists and Congress. In 1954-55 Pakistan joined the Southeast Asia Treaty Organization and the Baghdad Pact, and accepted substantial military aid from the United States. Pakistan's involvement in the American worldwide scheme for containment of the communist bloc was denounced by Nehru as bringing the Cold War to a neutral zone. He also suspected that the Pakistanis would use their new weapons to make a second attempt to overrun Kashmir.

But attempts to exclude the influence of external great powers from the affairs of the subcontinent were doomed to failure. The Indian Ocean and the north of India were far too important. As relations between the Soviet Union and the Chinese People's Republic deteriorated in the late 1950s, the Soviets took an increasing interest in north Kashmir. Their ideal would have been to control the area themselves, thus gaining access to India, and isolating China from central Asia. However, they were content to have Kashmir under Indian control as a means of excluding the Chinese.

In 1959 Pakistan proposed an Indo-Pakistani Defense Pact covering north Kashmir, to exclude the Soviet Union and the Chinese People's Republic. But Nehru considered such an arrangement unnecessary and provocative. India was on good terms with both China and Russia. In fact, the only source of threat, or object of hostility, was Pakistan. The Pakistanis concluded that it was impossible to achieve any arrangement with India. In 1962 the successful Chinese attack on India shattered Nehru's policy of nonalignment and had repercussions which contributed to the Indo-Pakistan War of 1965.

After 1962 the Indian Army was built up, and India accepted help from the United States and the Soviet Union. India now needed one army to watch Pakistan, and another to guard against the threat from China. The new divisions added to the Indian Army were of mountain troops, and not suitable for an invasion of Pakistan. However, the Pakistanis felt that Indian rearmament increased the threat against them. At the same time, the success of the Chinese attacks convinced some Pakistani leaders that India was not capable of fighting efficiently. Pakistan saw China as a potential ally against India.

The build-up to war

However, it was events in Kashmir that were the immediate cause of the 1965 War. In late 1962/early 1963 there were renewed talks on Kashmir, but the issues were the same, and so were the attitudes of the two governments. India proposed recognition of the *status quo* and a mutual withdrawal of forces. Pakistan demanded that there should be a vote held under international control. After the failure of these talks the Pakistanis convinced themselves that India, although basically weak and divided, was planning to attack Pakistan to settle the Kashmir question.

THE FRAGMENTED SUBCONTINENT **39**

The government began a "Hate India" propaganda campaign to prepare the masses for war. The Indians proceeded with the absorption of Kashmir, and in December 1964 claimed that it had been fully integrated into India. This was absolutely unacceptable to Pakistan. Meanwhile, there was considerable unrest inside Kashmir, caused by the corruption and brutality of the state authorities. Kashmiri rebels demanded the release of Sheikh Abdullah and a say in their own future.

The agitation in Kashmir persuaded Pakistan that there was an opportunity to expel India, and that it must be taken quickly, before the Indian Army got even stronger. In March 1965 Pakistan signed a Frontier Protocol and a Cultural Agreement with China. This greatly alarmed the Indian leaders, and they demanded more armaments from the Soviet Union. In both countries anxiety mounted to hysteria; the atmosphere was set for war.

The Indo-Pakistan War begins

The war of 1965 was short and indecisive. Militarily the result was a draw; politically no major issues were resolved. Despite the suspicions of the participants, there was no sign that either had made systematic plans to attack the other. Military policy on both sides was governed by opportunism, alarm and public hysteria. World opinion had no impact on the leaders. The United States and the Soviet Union were unable to prevent the war, but they did help to end it by cutting off supplies of military material to both sides.

On the Western Front, the opponents were almost equal. Overall, the Indian Army had a strength of 17 divisions, but had to employ some to watch the Chinese frontier, and some to cover East Pakistan, so only eight were available on the Western Front. Pakistan could field eight divisions of which seven were in the West, with one in the East Wing. India had three divisions in Kashmir, but these could be kept occupied by Muslim irregulars. On the rest of the Western Front five Indian divisions faced six Pakistani.

The Pakistanis enjoyed other advantages; their lines of communication were shorter, they had better tanks than the Indians, and more heavy artillery. The Indian Air Force could put up 500 aircraft against the 200 of the Pakistani Air Force. However, the Indian aircraft were of poor quality and its forces were widely dispersed. Pakistan had the more modern F-104 Starfighters and F-86 Sabres.

Indian soldiers move into defensive positions, taking their equipment, 1965.

Border clashes

The military action opened with minor skirmishes in the Rann of Kutch in spring. The Rann is a large area of marshy delta, flooded for half the year, extending inland from the northeast coast of the Arabian Sea. Although useless, the northern portion of it was claimed by both Pakistan and India, and both countries patrolled the disputed area in the dry season.

From January until April 1965, Indian and Pakistani frontier police met and clashed in this area. From April 10 until the annual floods arrived later in the month, the Pakistanis sent their army into the Rann, and took a number of Indian posts.

In May the Indians became concerned by the situation in Kashmir; they were worried by the possibility of infiltration by tribesmen from Azad Kashmir; they were very alarmed by the Pakistani protocol with China. Accordingly, Indian troops crossed the ceasefire line to take Pakistani posts in the Kargil area, to safeguard the strategic road north from Srinagar to Leh, their center of operations in Ladakh. They coincidentally obtained access routes into Azad Kashmir. To the Pakistanis these moves seemed to be preparations for an attempt to conquer Azad Kashmir. The Chinese encouraged Pakistan to make a really strong response.

The Gibraltar Forces

In June and July "Gibraltar Forces" were formed in Pakistan. These troops, some 30,000 in all, were a mixture of regular soldiers and volunteers, trained in the arts of guerrilla warfare. In August they went into Kashmir to raise the Kashmiris in a people's war of liberation against the Indian Army.

In the event, few Kashmiris were inspired to rise, but the Gibraltar Forces did inflict damage on economic targets and strategic roads, as well as harass the Indian Army. The Indian troops pushed them back toward their bases and crossed the ceasefire line. By mid-August they had made such progress that the Pakistani Army felt obliged to intervene directly to support the guerrillas, and launched a number of attacks across the ceasefire line. The Indians' reply was to threaten the Poonch-Uri area in southern Azad Kashmir with a pincer movement.

Pakistani prisoners captured in Kashmir being taken for interrogation, 1965.

The spread of war

As the Indian attacks made progress, the war spread southward. Operations grew in scale. On September 1 the Pakistani Army sent a force of tanks and infantry to push on the town of Akhnur, a bottleneck on the only road which the Indians had leading from Punjab into Kashmir. This operation, called "Grand Slam," could have isolated the Indian forces in Kashmir if it had succeeded. It did not succeed because the Indian Army made a number of thrusts in the Punjab, and from Rajasthan into Sind, to divert the Pakistanis.

The main Indian advances were on Lahore, of great political importance, and Sialkot, a center of communications vital to the Pakistanis. Neither of the thrusts reached its objective, but they led to extensive battles of 15 days' duration which absorbed the strength of the Pakistani Army in defensive operations. The tank battles around Sialkot were the largest since the Second World War.

The Pakistanis attempted to break the deadlock by sending a large armored force to advance on Amritsar. This column was lured into a strategic ambush, where dug-in tanks and antitank guns stopped it.

A Pakistani M47 tank under repair during fighting south of Lahore, September 1965.

Truce

By September 23 both sides had run out of energy and ideas, and both were short of tanks and ammunition. They yielded to the advice of the United Nations and the superpowers, and concluded a truce. This did not bring a complete end to the violence. In many areas local commanders indulged in minor operations to gain tactical advantages. The Indian High Command was reluctant to stop fighting, it wanted to eliminate the Pakistani military threat, and teach the Pakistanis a lesson. But the Indian government was content to have stopped the enemy offensives, and was afraid of Chinese intervention, so the war ended.

Neither side had gained a major advantage. Losses were similar, the extent of territory seized roughly the same, and no key points had been taken. The war proved that Pakistan and India were not capable of inflicting fatal wounds on each other. The central issue, that of Kashmir, remained unresolved.

In January 1966 the Indian and Pakistani leaders met at Tashkent, at a conference organized by the Soviet leader, Aleksey Kosygin. The Russians were anxious to halt the penetration of Chinese influence into Central Asia, and believed that China would gain most from further hostilities between India and Pakistan.

The Indians and Pakistanis accepted the prewar ceasefire line, disengaged their forces, and exchanged prisoners of war, but neither party modified its Kashmir policy. Both prepared to rearm. The Indians were convinced that Pakistan could be controlled only by deterrence. The Pakistanis saw this as a threat.

Politically, the war unified India, with a surge of mass patriotism. The political impact on Pakistan was divisive. The East Pakistanis were not particularly excited by the question of Kashmir, and resented being put at risk by the central government in the West. They found that their interests were very different from those of the West.

Bengali independence

In 1971 East Pakistan broke away to become Bangladesh. On the Western Front, the Indian forces inflicted a defeat on the Pakistanis. The defeat of 1971 shook the morale and political structure of Pakistan, so that subsequently it was preoccupied with internal difficulties and much less interested in renewed confrontation with India.

The civil war in Pakistan seemed almost inevitable, because the East Wing was so different from the West Wing. Unlike other parts of northern India, East Bengal had been converted to Islam by peaceful means. In the 15th century Bengal was taken into the Mughal Empire, and a ruling class of Urdu-speakers was imposed on the Bengali-speaking peasants. During the time prior to independence, Bengali Muslims often sided with Bengali Hindus, rather than in accordance with the policy of the League.

The partition of Bengal was bitterly resented, for cultural as well as economic reasons. After partition, East Pakistan was governed by mainly Urdu-speaking Westerners as well as some Bihari refugees. These rulers were alien to the Bengalis.

The geography, economy, history and traditional way of life of the Bengalis all combined to make East Pakistan very different from the West. Although the East had a larger population than the West, the national government was dominated by Westerners. After independence an Islamic constitution was agreed to in 1956, which was shortly after overturned when Ayub Khan imposed military rule. The imposition of military rule caused great offense in the East, which had a very strong commitment to the idea of democracy. The East was more productive than the West, but most of the money earned from exports was spent in the West.

The Awami League

A Bengali Muslim party, the Awami ("People's") League, emerged to give a voice to the East's grievances. Initially this party only wanted a program of reform but eventually it became a movement for separation. The Westerners' obsession with Kashmir was seen in the East as irrelevant and dangerous. Bengalis had no enthusiasm for war against India, and felt that if India were provoked, they would be more vulnerable to reprisals.

Flooding in East Pakistan following the cyclones which devastated the area in the winter of 1970.

In 1966 the Awami League put forward a manifesto of six points which demanded political and economic autonomy for the East. These demands could not be accepted by the national government, because it was strongly committed to the idea of national unity. However, by 1969 signs of discontent in the east were so menacing that the leader of the national government, General Yahya Khan, announced that he would change the constitution so that there would be one-man/one-vote. This meant that there would be a Bengali majority in the national assembly.

Electoral victory
In November 1970 East Pakistan was devastated by cyclones and floods, spreading destruction and misery everywhere. The national government was bitterly criticized for failing to provide quick and effective relief following the natural disaster.

In the elections held in 1970, the Awami League won a clear victory, and its leader, Sheikh Mujib Rahman, gained the right to be Prime Minister of Pakistan as a whole. This provoked a political crisis. Yahya and part of the army were in favor of making some concessions to the Awami League.

Right-wingers in the army and the leaders of the Pakistan People's Party, patriotic radicals led by Zulficar Ali Bhutto, who had won a majority in the West, did not agree. They saw the Awami League as a grave threat to the very survival of Pakistan. To them, Mujib and his followers were traitors. No compromise was possible, and unrest in the East mounted.

The army takes over
On March 25, 1971 the army took action to seize control of the East. Mujib and senior members of the Awami League were arrested. The East Pakistan Rifles, the local regiment, and the Bengali police were disarmed by force or attacked in case of resistance. Some were massacred. Elements of Bengali forces escaped, and fell back toward the borders with India, where they established defended enclaves.

On March 27 Major Zia, commander of one of these detachments, broadcast a declaration of independence. These armed refugees were welcomed and aided by India. The Indian people were very sympathetic to the Bengali cause. On April 10 a provisional government, established on Indian territory, proclaimed the independence of the new state of Bangladesh.

The Indian government was more cautious. Generally, the United Nations and world opinion took the view that affairs in East Bengal were an internal problem which Pakistan must be allowed to resolve without interference. The Chinese People's Republic's commitment to Pakistan was also a restraint.

In April, however, the Indian government started a diplomatic campaign in favor of intervention. This drew attention to violations of human rights in East Pakistan, which was under military rule. It also accused the Pakistani Army of crossing the borders into Indian territory, in its operations against the Bengalis, and emphasized the plight of the refugees.

Guerrilla warfare
The Pakistani government responded to this challenge. Yahya announced that a new constitution was to be drawn up, and once order had been restored, power would be transferred to civilian politicians. But political parties which were not "national" in outlook would be prohibited. Meanwhile the government agreed to accept United Nations' assistance to reconstruct the economy and resettle refugees.

By summer 1971 these measures were already irrelevant. Most Bengalis were determined to be free of Pakistan, and prepared to take violent action. They started with guerrilla actions. Small groups of Mukti Bahini guerrillas penetrated into East Bengal to attack and disrupt lines of communication.

The Indian government supported Bengali demands for self-determination. By early August the Indians had evidently decided that China would not act to preserve Pakistani control of the East. On August 9 India signed a Treaty of Peace, Friendship and Cooperation with the Soviet Union and prepared to give Bangladesh full support.

Under American pressure, Yahya made plans to hold elections, transfer power to civilian government, and allow the East to govern itself. But he would not release Sheikh Mujib, who was in jail in the West. The fate of the Sheikh became a major issue.

Pakistan tries to avert war
In October Yahya accused India of being responsible for the disorder in the East. He proposed a mutual withdrawal of forces from the frontier areas, and supervision of the East by UN observers. The Bangladeshi provisional government demanded the release of Sheikh Mujib, evacuation of the Pakistani Army, and immediate independence. India, with Soviet support, refused to accept UN observers and accused the Pakistani Army of posing a threat to Indian security.

The Pakistanis concluded that war against India was imminent. They took measures to try to deter the Indians. On the diplomatic level they sought moral support in the United Nations and called on China to help them. On the military level they prepared to defend the East against a conventional invasion, and assumed a threatening posture in the West. These measures failed.

The Indians knew that the Soviet Union would protect them within the United Nations. They were sure that China could not or would not intervene to preserve Pakistani control of the East, although the PLA would probably move if the survival of West Pakistan was endangered. The Indian armed forces were confident of being able to beat the Pakistanis in the East and the West.

Strengths and weaknesses

Late in October the Indian Army began to take part in the civil war, using artillery to keep Pakistani troops away from the frontier. In contrast to the random developments in 1965, in 1971 the Indian Army followed very clear plans in its operations against the Pakistani Army.

India enjoyed considerable advantages in this war. The substantial domestic armaments industry and the Soviet Union maintained a good supply of material. The Indian navy and air force were much larger and better equipped than their Pakistani equivalents. The Indian command structure was simple and effective, and relations between the services and the politicians were clear and cordial.

The Indian overall plan was to seek a quick victory in the East, and conduct a forward defense in the West. They had to wait until November when the monsoon (rainy season) was over and the ground hard enough for large-scale operations. Also the winter conditions meant the Chinese could not attack India directly.

Pakistan suffered a number of weaknesses. The country was still dependent on Western sources of arms. The command structure was complicated and too centralized, and military decisions were affected by political considerations. The loyalty of Bengali members of the forces was suspect, and their defection had a crippling effect on technical arms and services, especially in the air force. The Pakistani plan was to defend main centers in the East and go on the offensive in the West.

As Indian troops advance into Bangladesh, the refugees return home. Some six million Bengalis fled into India in 1971.

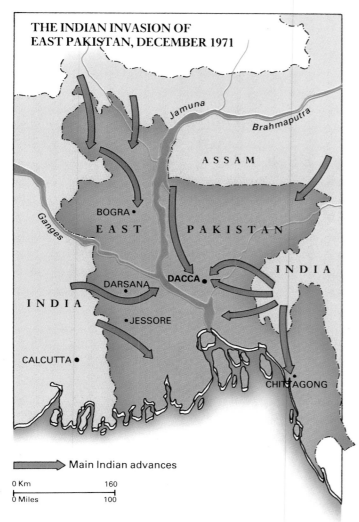

THE INDIAN INVASION OF
EAST PAKISTAN, DECEMBER 1971

Jamuna

Brahmaputra

ASSAM

Ganges

BOGRA •

E A S T   P A K I S T A N

DARSANA •

DACCA •

I N D I A

I N D I A

• JESSORE

CALCUTTA •

CHITTAGONG

➡ Main Indian advances

0 Km   160
0 Miles   100

Pakistan attacks

On December 3 major operations commenced in the West, with attacks by Pakistani ground and air forces. Attempts to catch the Indian Air Force by preemptive strikes on airfields failed, and the Indian response wiped out the Pakistani Air Force. Pakistani thrusts into Kashmir and Punjab were stopped, partly due to the Indian command of the air. By December 10 the Pakistani attacks had been stopped. Farther south, with the advantages of air support, the Indian Army advanced from Rajasthan into Sind, and overran the Rann of Kutch. It was clear that Pakistan could not influence events in the East by attacking in the West.

India advances

India recognized the Bangladeshi government on December 6. The Indian Army advanced into East Pakistan from three sides. The marshy terrain, in-tersected by water obstacles, was extremely difficult. The Indian Army showed great skill in the use of bridging teams, helicopters and aircraft to sustain rapid movements on foot. The Pakistani forces were trapped in the main centers, unable to move because of the difficult lines of communication, Indian air superiority, and the hostility of the rural population.

Six divisions of the Indian Army advanced, in conjunction with the Bangladeshi forces. By December 10 it was obvious that the Pakistani Army could not defend Dacca, capital of the East. On December 14 General Niazi, the Pakistani commander in the East, attempted to negotiate a ceasefire, but the Indian Army was intent upon total victory.

On December 16 the Pakistani forces in the East made an unconditional surrender. Although Yahya stated that the defeat in the East was merely a setback, and that the war would go on, Pakistan was not able to sustain a further effort. On December 17, India decided to halt operations and announced a ceasefire. Both the United States and China had made menacing moves.

Pakistani troops surrender, Dacca 1971.

Postwar relations

After 1971 relations between Pakistan and India improved. Having been soundly beaten and deprived of half its population, Pakistan could hardly be seen as a military threat to India. Conversely, India had not used its obvious advantage of strength to overrun and absorb Pakistan. The question of Kashmir was still of emotional importance, but Pakistan could not contemplate another attempt to resolve it by force.

The improvement in relations was helped by Mrs Indira Gandhi, who followed a conciliatory policy in dealing with Pakistan after the war. In July 1973 a conference at Simla agreed on a mutal withdrawal of forces. In August 1975 there was an agreement to exchange prisoners of war, and the Indians openly accepted that Pakistan had a right to exist. Pakistan recognized Bangladesh in February 1974.

In 1976 India and Pakistan reestablished normal diplomatic relations and restored rail and air links. The governments of both countries have endeavored to avoid conflict, but some difficulty is inevitable given the long history of bad relations in the past. Most recently, India has accused Pakistan of harboring and training Sikh terrorists.

Internal instability in Pakistan

Since independence Pakistan has been disturbed by a number of conflicts which have led to political instability. Separatist movements have been active, particularly in East Pakistan, but also in Baluchistan and the Northwest Frontier province. This last has assumed a greater importance since the Russian invasion of Afghanistan in December 1979.

The people have also been divided by conflicts of opinion between Westernized intellectuals and fundamentalist Muslim clergy, some of them influenced by developments in Iran. Disputes over the interpretation of religious ideas strike at the very heart of the idea of the country of Pakistan.

Because of the lack of other effective unifying forces, and the constant sense of external threat from India, the army has been particularly important in Pakistani politics. On successive occasions it has taken power when civilian politicians have reduced the country to disorder. The founder of Pakistan, Mohammed Ali Jinnah, died in 1948, of tuberculosis. In 1951 his successor, Liaquat Ali Khan, was assassinated. The loss of these two men deprived the country of competent and honest civilian political leadership.

The army took power in 1958 after the corruption and inefficiency of the civil government had led to widespread disorder. In 1971, after the loss of the East, the military government was deposed, and Bhutto took power. But in 1977 there was extensive rioting after he was accused of election rigging and political murder. The army, led by General Zia Ul-Haq, took power again, and after being tried and convicted of murder, Bhutto was hanged. The army is still in power, still endlessly preparing to transfer power back to civilian politicians, and never feeling it safe to do so.

Indian problems

India has also been troubled by linguistic, cultural and religious differences and by political oppositions. Indian governments have frequently used armed force to deal with violent internal opponents. But India has still retained democratic forms of government, with the army and police subject to civil authority.

The separatist movements, those desiring some form of self-government, arose naturally, from the very diversity of the people of India, but some of them have been manipulated by foreign powers. In particular, the Chinese People's Republic has by turns stimulated or restrained guerrilla action by the Naga and Mizo tribes of the northeast. The Chinese have also sponsored the Naxalite communist movement in West Bengal.

Sikh independence

The most dangerous movements of all have been religious. From independence onward, some Sikhs – members of a sect, centered on the Punjab, who follow their own unique and particular form of religion – wished to form a separate, independent state. Agitation for the creation of "Khalistan" has gone on ever since, but reached new heights in the early 1980s when extremists, weary of a lack of progress, resorted to terrorism in support of their demands. At the time, they constituted less than two per cent of the total population of India, but their campaign of violent demonstrations, bombings and assassination threatened the stability of Mrs Indira Gandhi's government.

By 1984, the leader of the more extreme Sikhs, Jarnail Singh Bhindranwale, had set up his headquarters in the Sikh shrine known as the Golden Temple, in Amritsar, and it was from here that the government was openly defied. In response, Mrs Gandhi authorized military action, and on June 5, 1984 Indian Army units stormed the Temple, killing Bhindranwale and many of his supporters. To the Sikhs, this was an outrage which had to be avenged.

Jarnail Singh Bhindranwale, leader of the extremist Sikhs, addresses his followers, June 1983.

On October 31, Mrs Gandhi was assassinated by her own Sikh bodyguards, an event which led to widespread violent anti-Sikh riots throughout India. Rioting was particularly violent in Delhi, where the police just looked on. The government, led by Mrs Gandhi's son, Rajiv, only just survived. The Sikh struggle continues, with terrorists active in the Punjab and other areas of northern India.

There have been other cases of violence – for example, attacks on Bengalis settling as immigrants in Assam – but none so threatening as those created by the Sikh demands. Religious conviction divides the people and encourages political extremism. Congress has tried to educate the people and make India a unified, tolerant country, but it has yet to succeed.

The Tamils in Sri Lanka

Nor is India alone in facing such problems, for similar conditions of differences in race and religion account for insecurity in Sri Lanka (Ceylon). Sri Lanka gained independence from Britain in 1948, but has been troubled ever since by clashes over language and political rights between the Buddhist Sinhalese, who constitute two-thirds of the population, and the large minority of Hindu Tamils, who came originally from southern India. A Tamil guerrilla movement – the "Tamil Tigers" – is engaged in a savage struggle against government forces, aiming to create a separate Tamil state in the north of the island. By 1984, the trouble had degenerated into virtual civil war, with Tamils fleeing from the south and the government authorizing strong countermeasures to the guerrillas.

The future

Troubles such as those in India and Sri Lanka indicate the problems facing the subcontinent in the foreseeable future. The high emotions of religion have been translated into political demands which, if met, would lead to a break-up of existing countries, forcing governments to respond with forceful measures which do little to calm the violence. As disturbances continue, the chances of permanent solutions, based on tolerance and understanding, are reduced, but without such solutions, the stability of the region will suffer.

CONFLICT IN THE 20th CENTURY: APPENDICES

The countries of modern Asia are no strangers to violence. China emerged as a communist power only after years of revolutionary struggle, based on the ideas of Mao Tse-tung; Korea has been fought over and left split between North and South; India, Pakistan and Sri Lanka have all suffered the effects of internal trouble. In Pakistan the army has played a crucial role in national politics unlike the Indian Army, which has served its government loyally.

PERSONALITIES

Zulficar Ali Bhutto (1928-1979). Pakistani politician. Bhutto entered politics in the early 1950s, and joined the military government as a minister before founding his own Pakistan People's Party in 1967. He won an election in West Pakistan in 1970 and, following the break-up of West and East Pakistan in 1971, he ruled as president of Pakistan (1971-73), stepping down to become prime minister under the new constitution (1973-77). Overthrown by General Zia in 1977, Bhutto was sentenced to death for conspiracy and executed in 1979.

Chiang Kai-shek (1886-1975). Chinese soldier and statesman. Leader of the *Kuomintang* (Nationalist) Party from 1925, Chiang was dedicated to the

Zulficar Ali Bhutto

reunification of China. By the late 1920s, his chief opponents were the communists but, despite effective military campaigns against them in 1934-35, he was diverted from final victory by the Japanese invasion of China (1937). Until 1945, Chiang led Chinese forces against the Japanese, only to face renewed war with the communists (1945-49). Forced to flee to Taiwan in 1949, he ruled there until his death.

Indira Gandhi (1917-84). Indian politician. As daughter of Nehru, she was introduced to politics at an early age. Appointed minister of information (1964), she became prime minister of India two years later, consolidating her power with a landslide victory in 1971. Growing civil unrest forced her to declare a state of emergency in 1975, and this

Chiang Kai-shek

contributed to her defeat in 1977, but she recovered to win the election three years later. She was assassinated by her own Sikh bodyguards on October 31, 1984.

Mohandas Karamchand Gandhi (1869-1948). Indian religious and political leader, known as *Mahatma* ("great sage"). After qualifying as a lawyer in London (1899), he worked in South Africa until 1913, when he returned to India intent upon the cause of independence from British rule. He advocated policies of non-violent protest and "civil disobedience." He played a leading role in the negotiations which led to India's independence (1947), but was assassinated by Hindu extremists on January 30, 1948.

Hirohito (1901-   ). Emperor of Japan since 1926. Until 1945, Hirohito was regarded as a god by his people, keeping aloof from politics. His role was altered under the American-imposed constitution of Japan (1946) and he is now no more than a figurehead.

Mohammed Ali Jinnah (1876-1948). First ruler ("governor-general") of independent Pakistan. Entering Indian politics in 1906, Jinnah became president of the Muslim League 10 years later. He was prepared to work with the Hindu-backed Indian National Congress to gain independence for India as a whole. But deep divisions between Hindu and Muslim sects forced him to accept the reality of a split between Pakistan and India in 1947. He died in September 1948.

Mao Tse-tung (1893-1976). Chinese communist leader. An early member of the Chinese Communist Party, Mao believed that true revolution could only come from the peasants. He created a "safe base" in the Kiangsi province (1927), but was forced to withdraw to Shensi (the "Long March," 1934-35) by military pressure from Chiang Kai-shek's *Kuomintang*. During the Sino-Japanese War (1937-45), Mao built up an army which reopened the conflict with the *Kuomintang* and achieved final communist victory. He created the People's Republic in October 1949 and was effective ruler of China until his death.

Yasuhiro Nakasone (1917-   ). Japanese politician. Nakasone entered politics as a member of the House of Representatives before becoming chairman of the National Organization of the Liberal-Democratic Party. Appointed minister of transport in 1967, he held a variety of ministerial and party posts in the 1970s, with special reference to trade and manpower services. He became prime minister of Japan in November 1982.

Jawaharlal Nehru (1889-1964). Indian politician. Educated in England, Nehru studied law in India before becoming a dedicated follower of *Mahatma* Gandhi. He joined the Indian National Congress

Mao Tse-tung

in 1918, and although he did not share Gandhi's belief in non-violent protest, he remained a loyal supporter of the campaign to gain independence for India. Appointed prime minister of India in 1947, he remained in power until his death, facing the immense problems of independence with some success.

Sun Yat-sen (1866-1925). Chinese revolutionary politician. Born near Canton but educated abroad, Sun was involved in plots against the Emperor's rule in China as early as the 1890s. In 1911, when the Manchu dynasty was overthrown, Sun served briefly as president of the new republic before being ousted by military men. Moving south, he formed a breakaway republic, based

on the socialist principles of his *Kuomintang* Party. He died before any success in the reunification of China had been achieved.

Teng Hsiao-ping (1904-   ). Chinese politician. An early communist, Teng took part in the "Long March" (1934-35) and was a political commissar during the wars against Japan (1937-45) and the *Kuomintang* (1945-49). By 1955 he was a member of the ruling Politburo, but he was removed from office during the Cultural Revolution (1967). He recovered to become chief of the general staff in 1975, only to be "disgraced" again a year later. In 1977 he returned to political office, eventually becoming chairman of the Communist Party (and effective ruler of China) in 1982.

General Mohammad Zia Ul-Haq (1924-   ). Pakistani army officer. After active service in the Second World War, Zia spent nearly 20 years in various staff and instructional posts, gradually rising through the officer ranks of the Pakistani Army. By 1969 he was a brigadier in command of an armored brigade; by 1975 he was a lieutenant-general in command of a corps. Appointed chief of the army staff in 1976, he took part in the coup which ousted Zulficar Ali Bhutto in 1977, assuming the presidency of Pakistan in September 1978.

Jawaharlal Nehru

Teng Hsiao-ping

Zia Ul-Haq

CHINESE REVOLUTIONARY WARFARE

When the Chinese communist leader Mao Tse-tung established the People's Republic in Peking in October 1949, it represented the culmination of a remarkable revolution. Only 22 years earlier, Mao had been confined to a small area in Kiangsi province, fighting for survival against seemingly overwhelming odds.

The key to Mao's success lay in his unique approach to the process of revolution. Central to his ideas was a firm belief that political change in China could only come through the peasants in the countryside, so his first priority had to be to find some way of persuading them to support the communist cause. Here Mao used his own experience to good effect. Having been born into the peasant class, he understood the realities of poverty and harsh rule, yet had escaped from them through education. Being a trained teacher, he could offer to the peasants and their children all the promises of education, gaining their support for something which they valued.

Setting up base areas

In the process, he would not only start to organize the people but also spread the communist word through reading or writing exercises. Once that occurred, the people could be persuaded to accept new forms of taxation and justice, based on the communist model but infinitely preferable to those which then existed. Gradually, an "alternative" society would be created, under communist control and in defiance of the Kuomintang or local warlords (the so-called "reactionary forces").

Obviously, this was not something that could be done openly, so Mao chose "base areas" which were remote and inaccessible. He hoped that the "reactionaries" would be unaware of what was going on.

The organization phase

Moreover, once a single base had been set up, selected leaders from within it would be sent into neighboring areas to repeat the process. Mao likened it to ink on blotting paper: just as a single spot of ink spreads until it is absorbed, so the revolutionary bases would spread over the countryside, isolating the cities and preparing the way for a takeover of political power by the communists.

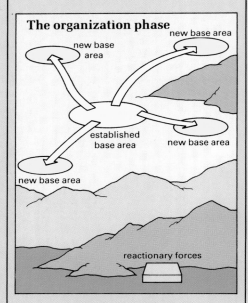

The organization phase

new base area

new base area

established base area

new base area

new base area

reactionary forces

This became known as the "organization phase" of the revolution and was vital to eventual success. Once the base areas were firmly established then the communists were in a powerful position and could defend themselves against opponents.

However, it was unlikely that "reactionary forces" would remain ignorant indefinitely, particularly if communist attempts to introduce new tax systems denied them money or they suddenly found that local people were defying existing laws. Faced with this danger, Mao's next stage was to search for ways to defend his bases as they developed.

Defending the bases

Quite clearly, he could not expect the peasants to form military units capable of fighting Kuomintang or warlord armies in open battle, but this did not mean that they were unable to take military action.

The peasants enjoyed two priceless advantages which their enemies could not match – an intimate knowledge of local terrain and support from the local population. Thus, if their base should be threatened, they could be formed into guerrilla groups and used to mount hit-and-run attacks on enemy units which had no local knowledge and no local support.

Any attempt to pursue the

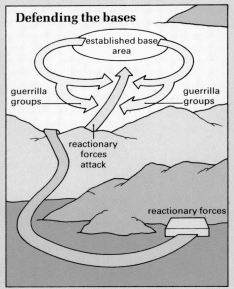

Defending the bases

established base area

guerrilla groups

guerrilla groups

reactionary forces attack

reactionary forces

guerrillas would draw the enemy into inhospitable areas in which further attacks could take place, while the guerrillas themselves would melt into the local population and be impossible to find. After a time, the enemy would become frustrated and demoralized, leaving the communists free to continue their political organization.

Guerrilla warfare

Admittedly, the enemy might respond by lashing out with massive force, killing the population and burning villages in a desperate attempt to root out the guerrilla groups.

But even this could be used to advantage by the communists, who could claim that it was another example of harsh rule by the *Kuomintang* or warlords.

At the same time, the guerrillas could survive by withdrawing from the area – a policy put into effect by Mao during the "Long March" of 1934-35. The enemy would concentrate on one location so that bases could be established elsewhere. As these new bases would also produce guerrilla groups of their own, the enemy would be faced with an epidemic of communist activity. For obvious reasons, this became known as the "guerrilla warfare phase."

Guerrilla warfare phase

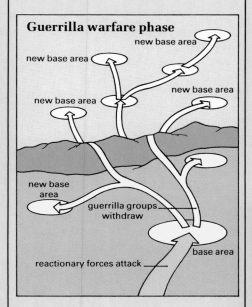

Protracted war

All this was likely to take time to effect – indeed, one of the central features of Mao's theory was the concept of "protracted war," sacrificing territory whenever necessary in order to gain time, and using that time to persuade the people to support the revolution. However, the final stages could be quite rapid. As the guerrilla groups gained in strength and prestige, their attacks would become more frequent and widespread. The enemy would then be forced to thin out his units in an attempt to cope. This would increase the demoralization of the enemy units as the soldiers within them were

Protracted warfare

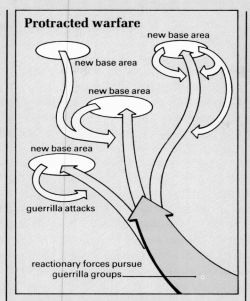

subjected to surprise assaults.

The advantage would eventually tilt in favor of the revolutionaries – although weak to begin with, their new-found effectiveness, combined with the diminishing strength of the enemy, would gradually give them the edge. Once that happened, the guerrilla groups could join forces to create a large conventional army, fully capable of defeating the

remnants of the enemy force in open battle. Known as the "open, or mobile, phase" of the revolution, this is exactly what happened in China during the Civil War (1945-49).

Seizing power

But this was only a means to an end, for the defeat of the enemy in battle would open the way to the realization of Mao's ultimate aim – the seizure of political power. A period of consolidation would then occur, during which the last vestiges of the old regime were rooted out and a communist system imposed. Through a careful process of organization, guerrilla attacks and open warfare, the will of the people, expressed through the ideals of communism, would be satisfied. It was a remarkable pattern of events and one which enjoyed success in China, and although it may be tempting to see Mao's "theory" as nothing more than a retrospective description of that success, there can be no doubt that it acted as a model for similar revolutions in areas as far afield as Vietnam (1945-75) and Cuba (1956-59).

Chinese guerrillas place a booby-trap device under a stool.

CHINESE TACTICS IN KOREA

The tactics employed by the Chinese forces in Korea (1950-53) were devised to counteract their enemies' advantages in firepower, mobility, airpower and technology. The Chinese also wanted to make best use of their own advantages: huge superiority of numbers, the enthusiasm of their soldiers and their ability to surprise the enemy.

Ambush
The most favored form of attack was the ambush of an unsuspecting enemy. Formal attacks on enemies in position were less favored. When they were necessary it was imperative to achieve surprise, surround the enemy and attack with a massive superiority of numbers.

Most attacks were made at night in order to avert the effects of the United Nations (UN) Forces' command of the air and superior firepower. There was constant use of deception to secure surprise and effective measures to deprive the enemy of information.

Defense of ground was held to be generally disadvantageous, but the particular circumstances in Korea forced Chinese troops to stand and fight for key areas. When they were required to defend, Chinese troops put great faith in deep and elaborate trench systems.

In between large-scale operations, the Chinese tried to dominate no-man's-land and to maintain their own morale by vigorous patrolling and raiding. The individual soldiers were expert in moving over terrain undetected. They frequently sent out substantial fighting patrols in order to catch unwary UN patrols.

Planning an attack
In the event of a formal attack, the smallest force to be employed by the Chinese would be a regiment of 3,000 men, divided into three battalions. Usually one battalion would lead the assault, followed closely by the other two as the second wave. Any formal attack would take place only after careful preparation and planning.

During this phase, the command staff would build up hidden supply dumps close to the battle area and gather as much information as possible about the enemy, using reconnaissance, observation and other means. The troops would then rehearse the attack over similar terrain far away from the objective.

Once the weakest point in the enemy's position had been identified, the staff would draw up a plan to attack it from at least two directions at once. The plan would also provide for numerous smaller attacks to confuse the enemy, and for the infiltration of forces to isolate the enemy from reinforcement and re-supply.

The aim would be to assault the enemy from as close as possible. If the troops could "embrace the enemy," they could inhibit his use of firepower. For such an attack to succeed, it was reckoned essential to outnumber the enemy by at least six to one.

The attack
Once the plan had been made, the attack would follow a standard pattern. During the preparation for the attack, forces would secretly encircle the objective (**1**) to flanks and rear, infiltrating deep to block all access. At the same time, the artillery would seek out the target, this process being generally concealed by an increase of harassing fire along a wide sector of the front line (**2**).

Encircling the objective

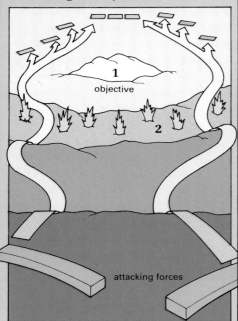

The approach

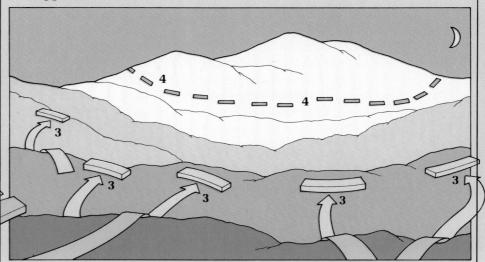

The approach would be made by the infantry, generally under cover of twilight, to "assembly areas" (**3**), 1-3 km (.5-1.5 miles) from the objective (**4**). This move would be made without the benefit of artillery to ensure surprise.

In the attack, the infantry would move, by companies in arrowhead formation (**5**), to "forming-up points," preferably only 50 meters (yards) from the objective. During this stage, the artillery would bombard the enemy directly (**6**).

For the assault, the artillery, supported by all other weapons they could find, including anti-tank and anti-aircraft guns, heavy machine guns and mortars, would fire briefly at maximum rate. The infantry would rush in (**7**) from all sides of the enemy position holding their fire to preserve ammunition, which was always in short supply.

As soon as it was possible, each soldier would hurl grenades at the enemy position. Bunkers and rifle pits (**8**) would be cleared with grenades and bayonets. The infantry often made their final rush through their own artillery fire, the justification being that their artillery would inflict fewer casualties than enemy machine guns or rifles. The

rush would be accompanied by bugle-calls, drum-beats and shouts to demoralize the enemy.

If the first battalion was stopped, the second wave of two battalions would come up and rush in as quickly as possible. If the first battalion overran the enemy position, however, it would go in pursuit of enemy fugitives to press them on to the blocking forces (**9**). Meanwhile, the second-wave battalions (**10**) would come up to deal with the enemy position, seize prisoners, search bodies for documents, evacuate wounded, remove all weapons and material that were useful and carry away the dead.

Tactical weaknesses

These attacks could be very effective but could be easily broken up by determined defenders. Battlefield communication was rudimentary; at battalion and company level it would be by runner, bugle, whistle and voice. This meant that if a force was not able to carry out a plan according to schedule, it would lapse into confusion.

In defense, the Chinese selected positions very carefully, favoring hilltops and rear slopes, out of the

enemy's view. The dominant features of a stretch of ground would be picked out and occupied in strength. Then the digging would begin. Trenches, bunkers, tunnels, mortar pits and observation posts would all be connected by covered trenches.

To the rear, long trenches would provide for concealed resupply and reinforcements. The aim was to make the soldiers as safe as possible from the UN Forces' artillery and airpower.

Defense tactics

In the event of an attack or raid, the Chinese did not generally defend their positions with artillery or small-arms fire. The infantry would generally lie secure in their tunnels and bunkers, with only a few sentries forward.

As the enemy approached, they would be subjected to mortar fire to disrupt their progress and shake their morale. Sometimes this would be supplemented by heavy machine-gun fire. As the enemy approached the lip of the Chinese trench, the defending soldiers would throw a flurry of grenades and then make an immediate bayonet charge. It was usually very effective.

The attack

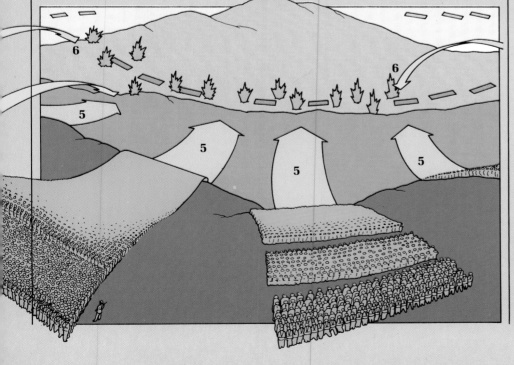

The assault

VIOLENCE ON THE INDIAN SUBCONTINENT

When the British withdrew from their Indian Empire in 1947-48, they left behind new countries already in the throes of internal violence, caused by a mixture of religious division and unsatisfied nationalism. The split between Hindu India and Muslim Pakistan was unsatisfactory, leaving many border areas in dispute between the two countries. The creation of Pakistan in two blocs (West and East) created the problem of how to rule a country separated by geography. Even in Ceylon (Sri Lanka), the situation was fraught with danger, caused by bitter splits between Buddhist Sinhalese and Hindu Tamils. In all cases, violence has erupted during the 40 years since independence, and although the following is by no means a complete list of religious or separatist groups in the sub-continent, it may be seen as representative of their extent and effects.

INDIA

Azad ("Free") Kashmir

The split between Hindu and Muslim populations in 1947 was not clear-cut, particularly in the north-western principality of Kashmir, ruled by a Hindu Maharaja yet containing a predominantly Muslim population. To begin with, the Maharaja tried to retain independence, but when elements of his people rose in revolt, he invited the Indians to intervene. In response, Muslim nationalists created *Azad Kashmir*, a politico-military movement dedicated to independence along Muslim lines. Lacking access to weapons, *Azad Kashmir* fighters adopted guerrilla tactics against the Indians, but failed to prevent a virtual takeover of the principality in 1948. They turned to Pakistan for aid, receiving training and arms, although in the process *Azad Kashmir* was absorbed into the Pakistani Army. By the late 1970s, it had ceased to exist as a separate entity.

Dal Khalsa

Founded on April 20, 1978, *Dal Khalsa* is a militant Sikh party – the "party of the pure" – which seeks independence for the Punjab province of India under the name of Khalistan. *Dal Khalsa* played a major role in the Hindu-Sikh troubles of 1982, after which it was officially banned. By then, it had attracted international attention when five of its members, armed with swords, hijacked an India Airlines Boeing 737 on a flight between New Delhi and Srinagar in September 1981.

Although swiftly overpowered, the hijackers demanded the release from detention of the Sikh sect leader Jarnail Singh Bhindranwale. He later took refuge in the Sikh holy place, the Golden Temple in Amritsar.

As Sikh extremism increased, Mrs Gandhi felt she had no choice but to commit Indian Army units to seize the Golden Temple, during which Bhindranwale was killed (June 1984). Hindu-Sikh violence resulted, culminating in the assassination of Mrs Gandhi (October 1984). The troubles still continue.

Naxalites

This is a collective term for extreme left-wing factions in India which emerged in the 1960s and mounted a series of terrorist actions until well into the 1980s. Centered on West Bengal, the Naxalites (so-called because their first armed attack happened in Naxalberi in 1967) are an off-shoot of the Indian Communist Party, believing in the Maoist pattern of rural guerrilla warfare.

Azad Kashmir *forces during a lull in the fighting, 1948.*

When this failed for want of peasant support in the late 1960s, the Naxalite leader, Charu Mozumdar, unleashed a "Red Terror" in Calcutta, killing policemen, members of the armed forces and wealthy "capitalists." Such actions helped to persuade Mrs Gandhi to declare a state of emergency in 1975, after which some negotiations began. However, by 1978 the violence had erupted again in Calcutta and this still continues, although on a reduced scale.

PAKISTAN

The Baluch People's Liberation Front (BPLF)
Dedicated to the creation of an independent state of Baluchistan in what is now western Pakistan, the BPLF emerged in 1976 out of the ashes of *Purari* (literally "grievances that cannot be settled through negotiation"). *Purari* had failed to gain political advantage from a rural guerrilla campaign in the early 1970s and many of its activists had fled over the border into Afghanistan, where the BPLF was formed. Guerrilla and terrorist operations continue, with cross-border infiltration from Afghanistan, but the long-running war in that country has tended to curtail Baluch activity. Since 1979, many Baluch extremists have taken to the hills of western Pakistan, intent on their own military actions, free from the dictates of a Soviet-dominated regime in Kabul.

Al-Zulficar Movement
This emerged in 1981 out of the remnants of the Pakistan Liberation Army (PLA), a group led by Murtaza Bhutto, son of the executed Pakistani leader, Zulficar Ali Bhutto. The PLA's aim was the overthrow of General Zia and it had carried out various acts of sabotage and terrorism in 1980. However it was destroyed from within by splits among its leaders, some of whom formed the Al-Zulficar Movement, with a similar aim, a year later. The Movement is backed by Libya's Colonel Gadaffi and by the pro-Soviet regime in Afghanistan, and has claimed responsibility for bomb attacks in Karachi (the chief port of Pakistan). Their aims became known internationally in February 1981, when members of the Movement hijacked a Pakistani airliner and held it for 10 days at Damascus (Syria), eventually securing the release of 55 detainees from Pakistan.

BANGLADESH

Mukti Bahini
This was created in early 1971 as an Indian-backed group dedicated to the elimination of West Pakistani rule over East Pakistan and the emergence of an independent Bangladesh. In late 1971 the West Pakistani commander in the East, Lieutenant-General Tikka Khan, ruthlessly cracked down on all opponents of Western rule. As units of the East Pakistan army mutinied, they formed the *Mukti Bahini* and conducted guerrilla attacks. Turning to India for aid, they prepared the way for the Indian invasion of December 1971 which led to the creation of Bangladesh. Thereafter, the *Mukti Bahini* was absorbed into the army of the new state.

SRI LANKA

Tamil Tigers
The split within Sri Lanka between the ruling Buddhist Sinhalese (in the south) and the Hindu Tamils (in the north) always promised violence. By 1976, a Tamil United Liberation Front (TULF) had been created, dedicated to the establishment of a separate Tamil state in the north of the island, and the Tamil Tigers (or Liberation Tigers) emerged as its more extreme wing in August 1977. A campaign of attacks against politicians and policemen began, leading to harsh measures from the government. As Tamils fled northward in the mid-1980s, protected by the Tigers, the island had come close to full-scale civil war.

Mukti Bahini *fighters prepare to go up to the war front, 1971.*

INDIAN ARMY

In 1947 the Indian Army contained 500,000 men, organized into regiments associated with local areas, on the British pattern. Most of the soldiers and nearly all the officers were from the "martial races," primarily from the Punjab and Northern Mountain regions. On partition, two-thirds of the old Indian Army was allocated to India.

The new army
The new Indian Army was 280,000 strong with good, trained volunteer long-service soldiers. This army proved itself effective in the fighting in Hyderabad and Kashmir in 1947-48. Thereafter, it was consistently neglected by the Indian government until the shock of the defeat by China in 1962.

The 1962 Campaign revealed grave deficiencies in the equipment, administration and command of the army. The government acted promptly. The high command was reorganized; the budget was raised to buy good equipment; the army doubled in size. Most of the new troops were put into mountain divisions to guard the frontier with China.

These measures were sufficient; in 1965 the army fought the Pakistanis to a stalemate; in 1971 it won a decisive victory. Since 1971, the army has been expanded further and now has a strength of 1.1 million.

The roles of the army
The roles of the army are, in order of priority, defense of the frontiers, internal security and support for the United Nations. The main deployments are on the frontiers with China and Pakistan to guard against invasion. Light forces aid paramilitary police formations, like the Assam Rifles, in containing tribal insurgents. The Naga rebellion started in 1956 and the Mizo tribes rose in 1966.

Until recently the army left internal security duties in the Indian heartland to the armed police, but in 1984, it was drawn into the struggle to suppress the Sikh militants and it was army units that assaulted the Golden Temple at Amritsar. This action had serious consequences as many Sikh soldiers mutinied in protest. The army has also served overseas in support of the UN, most notably in Korea, Zaire, West Irian and the Middle East.

Strength
The army can call upon some 180,000 regular reservists and 50,000 members of a volunteer, part-time Territorial Army. Attempts to create a mass militia of volunteers have had no success. In addition to the reserves, there are 175,000 men in the Assam Rifles and 85,000 in the Border Security Force, both paramilitary organizations.

In 1985 the army was organized into the following major formations:

2 Armored Divisions and 7 Independent Armored Brigades, with some 2,500 main battle tanks and 150 light tanks. The tanks were a mixture of Soviet T-54/55s and T-72s, as well as the Indian-made Vijanta, based on a British design (by Vickers).
1 Mechanized Infantry Division with some 850 Soviet armored personnel carriers (APCs).
19 Infantry Divisions and 10 Independent Infantry Brigades with Indian-made arms.
10 Mountain Divisions and 1 Independent Mountain Brigade, 1 Parachute Brigade.
8 Independent Artillery Brigades with very mixed equipment.
3 Engineer Brigades.

Indian troops cross a river in the Congo (Zaire) on a ferry, made by engineers, 1963.

PAKISTANI ARMY

The Pakistani Army started off at a disadvantage in 1947. It acquired about a third of the soldiers of the old Indian Army but very few fully formed units. Further, most important arsenals, supply dumps and training establishments happened to be in India. This meant that the Pakistani Army was initially very reliant on British officers and lagged behind the Indians in equipment.

The primary role of the Pakistani Army has always been to ensure the survival of the state. From the outset, the state was menaced by external enemies on all sides. India was obviously the most important, but there has also been a constant threat of raids from Afghanistan.

Internal threats have also arisen. The most damaging of these was the East Bengali insurgency, which ended in military catastrophe for Pakistan in 1971. However, at least the loss of East Pakistan has simplified the strategic problems of defending the nation. Since the early 1970s the army has had to deal with separatists in Baluchistan. The army has also acted as guardian of the people against the consequences of the failure of civilian politics.

Finally, in recent years, the army has sent considerable numbers of soldiers abroad on contract to earn valuable foreign money and to consolidate a sense of Muslim solidarity. In the mid-1980s, some 30,000 Pakistani soldiers were serving in Saudi Arabia, Jordan, Oman, the United Arab Emirates and Libya.

Military rule

The army first took power in 1958. The country was lapsing into disorder due to the dishonesty and incompetence of civilian politicians. Ayub Khan restored order and experimented with a system of local "basic democracies."

A Pakistani tank recovery vehicle tows away a Centurion tank, 1965.

By 1968, official corruption had led to discontent and Ayub was replaced by Yahya Khan. Yahya's plans for constitutional reform were delayed and made futile by the loss of East Pakistan.

After the defeat of 1971, he was deposed and a civilian politican, Zulficar Ali Bhutto, a patriotic radical, took power. He created a Federal Democratic system of government, but in 1977 there was extensive rioting against his rigging of elections.

The army, led by Zia Ul-Haq, moved to depose Bhutto. The Military Government still rules in Pakistan, but it is threatened by the partisans of Mr Bhutto, led by his daughter, Benazir. However, it remains the most powerful institution in the country. No political party can match its discipline and organization or its prestige with the people.

Strength

The army has consistently expanded since formation to match the perceived threat from India. In the mid-1980s, defense accounted for 25-30 per cent of the National Budget and the army was larger than in 1971. Equipment is drawn from many foreign sources as Pakistan's own armaments industry is not yet fully developed.

In the mid-1980s, the army had the following major formations:

2 Armored Divisions, 4 Independent Armored Brigades and 6 Armored Reconnaissance Regiments. These hold a total of 1,500 American and Soviet tanks.
16 Infantry Divisions and 8 Independent Infantry Brigades with some 500 APCs.
3 Independent Artillery Brigades with a variety of British and Soviet guns of widely differing ages.
3 Brigades of Anti-aircraft Artillery and 7 Batteries of American Stinger, French Crotale and Chinese CSA-1 surface-to-air missiles (SAMs).
1 Special Services Group of infantry trained in infiltration, reconnaissance and sabotage techniques.

The regular strength of the army was 450,000 with a Regular Reserve of 500,000. In addition, there were some 164,000 paramilitary forces; and a National Guard of 75,000.

CHRONOLOGY

1921

July 1 Communist Party founded in China

1928

January Chiang Kai-shek establishes government at Nanking

August 7 Mao Tse-tung sets up the Red Army in China

1937

July 7 Sino-Japanese war begins

1941

December 7 Japanese attack on Pearl Harbor; Second World War in the Far East begins

1942

May 2 Congress starts "Non-cooperation" and "Quit India" campaigns

1945

August 6 and 9 Atomic attacks force Japan to surrender

August 9 Soviet forces overrun Manchuria

August-October Chinese Civil War begins

1946

January 1 Indian General election; Congress wins eight provinces; Muslim League wins three.

August 16 League "Direct Action Day;" riots in Calcutta

October 30 Massacres of Muslims in Bengal and Bihar

1947

August 15 Independence Day for India and Pakistan

October 22 Muslim irregulars invade Kashmir

October 26 India seizes Junagadh

November 2 Gilgit, Swat and Chitral join Pakistan

1948

February 4 Sri Lanka gains independence

February 6 Pakistani Army enters Kashmir

September 13-18 India occupies Hyderabad

October 20-November 4 Communists capture the cities of Manchuria

November 20-December 4 Kuomintang troops defeated around Hsuchow

December 31 Truce in Kashmir; Peking and Tientsin confined in a pocket by Red Army

1949

January 22 Peking surrenders to the Communists

October 1 Mao Tse-tung proclaims the Chinese People's Republic

1950

February 14 Sino-Soviet Alliance signed

June 25 North Korean Army attacks South Korea

July 27 North Koreans stopped on the Pusan perimeter

September 15 UN Forces make landings at Inchon

October 7 PLA invades Tibet

November 26 First contact between Chinese and South Korean Army

1951

September 8 US-Japan Defense Treaty

October 26 Main Chinese occupation force arrives in Tibet

1952

November 12 Sheikh Abdullah takes power in Kashmir

1953

July 27 Armistice in Korea

August 9 Sheikh Abdullah jailed by Indian authorities

1954

July 1 Foundation of the Japanese Self Defense Forces

September 8 Pakistan joins SEATO

November-December First Taiwan Strait crisis

1955

September 23 Pakistan joins the Baghdad Pact

1956

March Khamba uprising in Tibet

1958

August 6-October 23 Second Taiwan Strait crisis

October 7-8   Military government takes power in Pakistan

1959

January 3   National uprising in Tibet

March 17-30   Flight of the Dalai Lama from Tibet

1960

January 20   Kashmir brought under full Indian rule

1961

December 11   India seizes Goa from Portugal

1962

October 20-November 22   Sino-Indian war in Northern Kashmir and Himalayas; China begins to pursue territorial claims against the Soviet Union

December   Indo-Pakistani talks on Kashmir begin

1964

October 16   China tests an atomic bomb

December 4   India announces full absorption of Kashmir

1965

March 27   Sino-Pakistan Border Protocol and Cultural Agreement

April 9-29   Skirmishes in the Rann of Kutch

May 17   Indian Army seizes Pakistani posts in Northern Kashmir

August 5   Pakistani "Gibraltar Forces" go into action in Kashmir

September 1-23   Indo-Pakistani War

1966

January 4-10   Tashkent Conference decides Indo-Pakistani ceasefire

May   Cultural Revolution begins in China

June   Awami League demands autonomy for East Pakistan

1967

June 17   China tests a thermo-nuclear bomb

1969

March 26   Yahya Khan announces constitutional reforms for Pakistan

March   Sino-Soviet clash on Ussuri

April 24   Cultural Revolution ends

December 11   Ping-pong diplomacy begins

1970

November 13   Cyclones hit East Pakistan

December   Awami League wins elections in Pakistan

1971

March 25   Uprising in East Pakistan

April 10   Declaration of independence by Bangladesh (East Pakistan)

August 9   India signs friendship treaty with the Soviet Union

December 3-16   Indo-Pakistani War

December 18   Yahya Khan removed from power

1972

February 27   United States accepts that Taiwan is part of China

1973

August 28   Simla Conference; Indo-Pakistan relations normalized

1976

January 1   Japanese begin "Self Defense Build-up Program"

September 9   Mao Tse-tung dies; power struggle begins

1977

July 5   General Zia Ul-Haq seizes power in Pakistan

1979

January 1   United States formally recognizes the Chinese People's Republic

February 18-March 16   China attacks Vietnam

April 4   Bhutto hanged

December 24   Soviet invasion of Afghanistan

1980

January   China involved in supporting resistance to Soviet occupation of Afghanistan

1983

September 1   Korean jumbo jet shot down over Sakhalin

1984

June 6   Indian troops assault the Sikh Golden Temple in Amritsar

October 31   Mrs Ghandi assassinated by Sikhs; Communal violence

INDEX

Note: Numbers in bold refer to illustrations or maps

FURTHER READING

Acheson, D., *The Korean War* (Norton, 1971)

Akbar, M. J., *India: The Siege Within* (Penguin, 1985)

Chiu, H., *China and the Taiwan Issue* (Praeger, 1979)

Choudhury, G. W., *Pakistan's Relations with India, 1947-66* (Praeger, 1968)

Clubb, O., *Twentieth-Century China* (Columbia University Press, 1978)

Fraser, A., *The People's Liberation Army: Communist China's Armed Forces* (Crane Russak, 1973)

Gittings, J., *The Role of the Chinese Army* (Oxford University Press, 1967)

Griffiths, P., *Modern India* (E. Glastonbury, CT: Ind-US, Inc., 1962)

Hersey, J., *Hiroshima* (Knopf, 1946)

Kosaka, M., *One Hundred Million Japanese* (Kodansha, 1972)

Liu, C., *The Sino-Indian Border Dispute* (Westport, CT: Greenwood, 1986)

Liu, F. F., *A Military History of Modern China, 1924-1949* (Westport, CT: Greenwood, 1981)

Mao Tse-tung on Revolution and War, ed. M. Rejai (Magnolia, MA: Peter Smith, n.d.)

Murakami, H., *Japan, The Years of Trial, 1919-52* (Kodansha, 1983)

Nelson, H., *The Chinese Military System*, 2nd ed. (Boulder, CO; Westview, 1981)

Richardson, H., *Tibet and Its History* (Boston, MA: Shambhala, 1986)

Rustomji, N., *Imperilled Frontiers: India's North-Eastern Borderlines* (Oxford University Press, 1983)

Shieh, M. J. T., *The Kuomintang, Selected Historical Documents* (St. John's University Press, 1970)

Terrill, R., *Mao; A Biography* (Harper & Row, 1981)

Whitson, W. R., *The Military and Political Power in China in the 1970s* (Praeger, 1972)

Wilson, D., *When Tigers Fight: The Story of the Sino-Japanese War, 1937-1945* (Penguin, 1983)

(Note: All publishers located in New York unless specified otherwise.)

ACKNOWLEDGMENTS

Cover: Salamander Books; contents page: Sally and Richard Greenhill; page 7: Oriental Department, British Library; page 8: BBC Hulton; page 9: Peter Newark's Western Americana; page 10-11: Time/Life – Colorific; page 12: Robert Hunt; page 14: Peter Newark; page 18: Robert Hunt; page 19: Robert Hunt; page 20: MARS; page 21 (top): Popperfoto; page 21 (bottom): UPI/Bettman Archives; page 22: Larry Burrows/ Colorific; page 26: Sally and Richard Greenhill; page 27: Sally and Richard Greenhill; page 28: The Research House (TRH); page 30: Colorific; page 33: Photosource/Keystone; pages 34-35: RMA Sandhurst; page 38: Photosource/Keystone; page 39: Robert Hunt; page 40: Robert Hunt; page 41: Popperfoto; page 42: Tom Learmonth; page 44: Photosource/Central Press; page 44 (inset): TRH; page 45: Popperfoto; page 47: Rex Features; page 48 (top): Robert Hunt; page 48 (bottom): BBC Hulton; page 49 (top): Popperfoto; page 49 (left): BBC Hulton; page 49 (center): Photosource/Keystone; page 49 (right): Photosource/Central Press; page 51: Popperfoto; page 54: Popperfoto; page 55: Popperfoto; page 56: Popperfoto; page 57: Robert Hunt.